JAPANESE BUDDHISM

JAPANESE BUDDHISM

A Critical Appraisal

by

WATANABE Shoko

KOKUSAI BUNKA SHINKOKAI

(Japanese Cultural Society)

Tokyo, 1970

First edition, 1964
Revised edition, 1968
Third edition, 1970

Published by KOKUSAI BUNKA SHINKOKAI, *1-1-18, Shirokanedai, Minato-ku, Tokyo (108), Japan. Distributed by* JAPAN PUBLICATIONS TRADING CO. LTD. *P.O. Box 5030, Tokyo International, Tokyo, Japan; P.O. Box 7752 Rincon Annex, San Francisco, Calif., 94103, U.S.A.; Paul Flesch & Co. Pty. Ltd. 259 Collins Street, Melbourne, Australia, 3000.* © *1970 by Kokusai Bunka Shinkokai; all rights reserved.*
Printed in Japan, by General Printing Co., Ltd., Yokohama

LC Card No. 70-110946

It has long been regretted that students and scholars who engage in Japanese studies have to face many difficulties, not only in having to master a difficult language, but also in the matter of the lack of effective assistance by the learned institutions and people of this country. Recognizing this fact, the Kokusai Bunka Shinkokai (Japan Cultural Society), since shortly after its establishment in 1934, has been applying its energies to several programs for providing such facilities for foreign students and friends of Japan.

Initially the Society made a collection of Western-language books and magazines relating to Japan, which are available for reference at the K.B.S. Library, and published a full catalogue of the items collected during the years 1935–62, *A Classified List of Books in Western Languages Relating to Japan,* which is obtainable from the University of Tokyo Press.

Concurrently, since 1959 the Society has been compiling a series of bibliographies, under the series title *A Bibliography of Standard Reference Books for Japanese Studies with Descriptive Notes,* listing and describing the more important books written on Japan in Japanese. This is proving another valuable contribution to Japanese studies. Volumes already published cover the following fields: Generalia, Geography and Travel, History and Biography, Religion, History of Thought, Education, Language, Literature, Arts and Crafts, Theatre-Dance-Music, Manners and Customs and Folklore, Politics, Law, and Economics. Supplementary volumes will appear successively.

Since 1961 the Society has also been publishing a series of books on Japanese life and culture, including the present publication, which give basic guidance in introductory fields of Japanese studies. Out of more than fifteen such published studies, the Society has now selected a number, as listed on the last pages of this volume, which have been revised and reissued. More volumes, both revised and original editions, will appear successively. It is the sincere hope of the Society that this series, as well as its other activities, may prove of value to all who are interested in the study of Japan.

Buddhism was introduced into Japan more than fourteen centuries ago, since which time it has undergone many modifications. In spite of these changes, however, it has retained its basic principles and practices, while at the same time it has become very much a distinctive religion of the Japanese people.

The present book, by Dr. WATANABE Shoko, Professor of Buddhism at Tôyô University, is designed to present a general view of this religion for the benefit of foreign students of Japanese culture. It is based on a work that was originally published by Iwanami Shoten in its series *Iwanami Shinsho* (New Books of Iwanami). Its appearance in English translation is due to the courtesy of the publisher and to the kindness of the author, who rearranged some of the material for this special purpose.

Thanks are also due to Dr. Alfred Bloom, of the University of Oregon, for his translation of the text, and to Dr. William P. Woodard, for helpful suggestions in editing the manuscript.

December, 1970   Kokusai Bunka Shinkokai

Contents

viii

It is impossible to consider the life of the Japanese and leave out Buddhism. This is obvious from past history, and it is also the case for our own times. However, it is not easy to survey Japanese Buddhism. The reason is that since complex Japanese Buddhism, such as we see at present, was constituted by various elements, mutually important and intertwined, we cannot understand its actual condition unless we make clear its constituents. Besides this, to make matters worse, it is increasingly difficult to have an unobstructed view of the whole of Japanese Buddhism, because there are too many propagandistic books centered in the standpoint of particular sects.

We have endeavored to make clear the logic which indicates how Buddhism, as an imported, foreign thought, was adopted, understood and practiced in Japan from the historical standpoint that Buddhism, which had been developed in India, was transformed in China, and transmitted to Japan. At the same time, we have tried to consider the question of how the thought and customs peculiar to the Japanese caused Buddhism to be transformed. Thus, in addition to reducing it to its various elements, we have explained the process by which Japanese Buddhism was formed. Here we find expressions of profound religious and philosophical thought and a high ideal of human love; but there are also some distorted views and a despicable professionalism. If we consider that there are both famous priests of high scholarship and rich in the power of execution, and saintly priests who merged with the people, there are also phoney teachers who aimed at reputation and authority and misled the people. Also there are the "high priests" (*kôsô*) who, although they possessed expressly good intentions, asserted absurd ideas because a fundamental knowledge of Buddhism was lacking. Although both may similarly be called temples, there are sacred places of religious endeavor, and there are also those which are only places for amusements such as sightseeing and picnicking. In a word, things of every degree, running the whole gamut, are present in Japanese Buddhism. It is not unwarranted that on seeing this a person is bewildered.

"If you hate a monk, hate even his surplice (kesa)." We frankly recognize also that unpleasant aspects certainly exist in Japanese Buddhism. However, to tell the truth, there are many strong points to the extent that there is no comparison. We would like to have the person, who would dislike without tasting, taste one mouthful. Therefore, we have laid bare, without hesitation, the strong and weak points of Japanese Buddhism, and picking these out, we have produced a menu. It is this book. We planned to take up in a general way the issues which appear necessary for understanding the present condition of Japanese Buddhism; but, there was no room at all to touch on the influence which Buddhism exerted on literature and art. This would be a subject for a separate book.

Because of proneness to a parochial nationalism and an excess of sectarian consciousness since the Meiji period, a fairly atrocious self-praise has come to reign supreme concerning the form of Buddhism characteristic of Japan. This was not a conclusion based on objective judgment, but frequently only sentimental dogma. It is necessary to balance accounts at the present time when the level of Buddhist research has come to be elevated worldwide. There is nothing to be proud of in just saying "original." It will only be a subjective judgment, if we do not make clear such questions as: What kind of position does it occupy in the history of world thought? How much influence has it exerted actually on men and society?

When we look critically from such a perspective, we cannot say that priests who became famous in history were necessarily great Buddhists. There are not a few problems in the value judgments which, since Meiji, were long ago taken as accepted theory. If we do not make these points clear, we cannot grasp the essential nature of Japanese Buddhism. There are things written in this book which are in considerable contradiction with previously accepted theory. However, we are not relating our own individual thought. We are only bringing together logically the historical facts and the results of the research of reliable domestic and foreign scholars. On individual points there are also treatises which we have published before now, and hereafter also we intend to discuss them whenever there is an opportunity.

January, 1958   WATANABE Shoko

When Arnold Toynbee visited Japan, one of the things that interested him was the question of to what extent Buddhism had played a part in the Japanese way of life. However, it appears that the answer of Japanese scholars to his question was frequently negative. A similar interest was possessed by the foreigners who gathered in 1957 for the International Pen Convention; but there does not appear to have been, on the side of the Japanese, persons to make a satisfactory reply. It appears by no means rare that not only historians and literary scholars, but also foreigners coming to Japan, make an issue of the relation of the Japanese people and Buddhism, whereas it is not infrequent that the Japanese himself, at least on the surface, is disinterested.

Indeed, may it not be that Buddhism no longer is living in the Japanese way of life? Actually, there are not a few intellectuals who think so. No matter what sphere one considers, politics, economics, society or culture, we can say from the start that Buddhism never appears externally influential. Articles related to Buddhism are extremely few in news reports and general publications. On this point, the growth of a new sect, the *Sôka Gakkai,* in the past five or six years is remarkable. However, it is also a fact that the latent power of Buddhism cannot be treated lightly. Even now, the greater part of the Japanese are, at least formally, Buddhists. They are each registered as the parishioner or believer of some temple and some sect, and when there is occasion, they will participate in religious ceremonies. In most homes rites related to Buddhism are performed. That Buddhism has influence also in the sphere of actual society appears in the economic strength of the great temples and sects. We cannot treat lightly either, the institutions which they administer (education and social work). Looking at it politically, it is a fact that a good number of votes in an election are gathered with the Buddhist organizations in the background. Actually, in the Meiji and Taishô eras the priests were not eligible for election because their political growth was feared.

In the cultural sphere, also, Buddhism was completely shut out of school education through the policy of the Meiji government and it was looked upon as something conservative and retrogressive by those advocates of Western European progressivism. However, Buddhism, which we may say received a double attack, front and back, did not disappear from the life of the common people.

From another angle, interest in Buddhism gradually heightened in Europe and America. During the period of spiritual upheaval following the First World War, *The Decline of the West* (Spengler) was being intoned, but after the Second World War there appeared the positive effort which anticipated the future development of mankind through the union of Western and Oriental cultures. Here Buddhism came to have great significance. But though we speak of Buddhism, the main interest of Western Europe from the nineteenth century was directed to *Theravada* Buddhism (so-called *Hinayana*) or Tibetan and Mongolian *Lamaism*. However, more recently the Buddhism of East Asia, particularly that of Japan, has attracted wide attention. The reason for this is that almost every aspect of Buddhism can be found in Japan in contrast with the fact that the forms of Buddhism in the other regions transmit only one aspect of that religion. Besides this, the question of whether an ancient religion is actually alive in modernized Japan has a fascination for Europeans and Americans. Thus it is a fact which appears beyond doubt that at present Japanese Buddhism is drawing the attention of the world.

What was Japanese Buddhism like in the past? To what extent is it living in the present? Such questions must be considered more penetratingly. But these points are disregarded because, although people in general seek the significance of Buddhism in relation to their lives, specialists discuss only the doctrines and traditions within religious organiza-

tions which have only a faint relation to the question of the relation of
Buddhism to everyday life. There is a mutual discrepancy here. By all
means we must investigate the inter-relation of Buddhism and Japanese
life, past and present, at the points where they are directly linked in
actual life. And for this we must examine what is Japanese and what is
Buddhist from various angles and a broader perspective. We must not
be defensive of doctrine, but we must discern, not merely with objective
observations, but the inward aspects.

The methodology of the natural sciences since the end of the nineteenth century has had great influence on the cultural sciences and
particularly on the study of the history of religions also.

Even in the study of the life of Jesus Christ, it was once fashionable to
construct an image such as would suit the sensibilities of modern man
by depicting only elements which appeared rational. There was a period
when such a tendency was strong even in the study of Buddhism.
However, later, along with progress in the study of the history of religion
and religious psychology, the necessity for an original method was emphasized in the sphere of the study of religion: that is to say, a method
of grasping the phenomenon called religion in its inner laws and making
clear its special characteristics as a social phenomenon. The result is that
various interesting publications and treatises have appeared during the
last ten years on the many religions of India and particularly Buddhism.
It appears that such types of research are comparatively few in number
only in research in Japanese Buddhism. Keeping this in mind, it is the
aim of this book to inquire into such questions as: What was Japanese
Buddhism in the past? What are the reasons for its present condition?
What may we expect in the future? In choosing to consider these questions, the most important thing is to observe the facts as they are and
leave aside prejudice. It is to strive as far as possible to revive the way of
thought and life of the society and age which are the objects of our
observations. It is obviously impossible to understand the past if we
consider trying to speculate on all of past history with the narrow experience of our generation of hardly fifty or sixty years, and it will be
impossible also to grasp sufficiently the shape of the contemporary age.

Indeed, since it is one of the achievements of the twentieth century that such a method of historical consciousness has been established, the method which we will employ here will also be extremely new.

Japanese Buddhism is an existence with which we have become too familiar, but it is also, at the same time, a blind spot which has not been properly evaluated up till now. We may call it, so to speak, one of the riddles of our own day. It is the plan of this book to discover the key for understanding that riddle in the historical facts of the past, while referring also to parallel examples elsewhere.

CHAPTER I

The Men Who Constructed Japanese Buddhism

Buddhism: An Imported Foreign Thought

In order to grasp the character of Japanese Buddhism, it is necessary to understand first of all that it is an imported religion. It is conspicuous throughout the whole of Japanese history that foreign thought always quickly influenced Japanese thought and action. Even now it is said that Paris modes are immediately reflected in New York and Tokyo. From ancient times Japanese have been very sensitive to foreign thought. It is not infrequent that the influence of foreign thought can be discerned even, for example, in nationalist thought that rejects foreign things, when the Japanese himself is not even conscious of it.

It is Buddhism that has exerted influence over the longest period of time and on the broadest scope among the influences of foreign thought in Japan. If we regard provisionally Ôjin Tennô's 16th year (285 A.D.) as the time of the popular transmission of Confucianism it is 250 years earlier than Buddhism. But if we take it from the standpoint of popular influence, none of the numerous foreign philosophies come up to Buddhism in influence or are as important for the Japanese as Buddhism. The result was very great, though it has plus and minus aspects. What kind of influence did Buddhism produce among the Japanese as a foreign thought? What was the Japanese attitude when they accepted it? Further, in what way did they alter that foreign thought? Such problems are not concerned with those of Buddhism alone. The reason is that the question of what kind of response the Japanese will make in the future toward Marxism, Christianity or American democracy is claiming the attention of people at home and abroad. All may expect to discover the key to predict the future in the past 1,500-year history of Japanese Buddhism.

The Mode of Reception of Buddhism

Japanese readiness to adopt foreign culture is not particularly new as is seen in the recent inflow of modernistic designs and French *chansons*. In about the middle of the sixth century, when the highest rulers of the Yamato court resided in primitive palaces (built directly on the ground without cornerstones), Buddhism, the essence of the culture of six dynasties (222 A.D.–589 A.D.) in China, which was the newest current from the continent, was actively adopted. Articles of art dating from the eighth century, are preserved chiefly in the Shôsôin (Imperial Repository) in Nara. Besides pictures and sculpture, various necessary articles, such as types of metal, wood, bamboo, lacquer, pottery, glass, dyed and woven objects, contain western elements from such places as Persia. They were transmitted through China and actually indicate a rich beauty. Because Chinese designs were imitated almost identically in Japan, frequently the imported articles cannot be distinguished. It may be said that this point also often applies to present-day Japanese productions. As is often said concerning Buddhist images, new styles of the continent soon influenced Japan and it is conspicuous that generally they underwent parallel changes especially to the beginning of the Heian period. Influence was always received in the art of making images as long as there was continued contact with the continent.

How is it in the sphere of thought? Thought was by no means received in the same manner as in the plastic arts. In the first place, the language barrier was a problem. Secondly, there were differences in thought, action and attitude toward life.

Buddhism was originally an Indian religion, but the Buddhism which the Japanese received was almost without exception Chinese Buddhism. Consequently, when we consider the reception of Buddhism, the problem only concerns Chinese Buddhism. In the first century of the Western era when Buddhism was introduced, the Chinese adopted a policy in receiving this foreign religion which adapted it to the existing conditions because there was already in China a highly developed language, literature, and philosophy. Later this policy was more or less modified. The

Chinese had a strong tendency to adopt all foreign culture, first absorbing it in their own manner. So they transformed the Indian elements in Buddhism in their own way. People will differ as to whether we call these transformations, distortions, or progressive developments, but, in any case, we must recognize that there are conspicuous differences between the thought of Indian and Chinese Buddhism.

Buddhism was transmitted to the Korean peninsula by way of some of the North Chinese countries, such as the Former Chin and Eastern Chin, from about the end of the fourth century. When the Wei dynasty was flourishing (5th century), Buddhism was spread domestically and abroad, parallel with the extension of their national power. Around the middle of the sixth century, Buddhism was transmitted to Japan from the Korean peninsula. We may view it more as the natural result of the expansion to foreign countries of Chinese culture than as a demand of Japan itself. In short, as water flows down hill, Chinese Buddhism flowed into Japan. Indian Buddhism which was the root of Chinese Buddhism existed in our fairly distant and inaccessible country, but in most cases it was nothing more than a conceptual existence rather than a real existence.

Because the direct mainspring of Japanese Buddhism was Chinese Buddhism, it was necessary first of all to learn the Chinese language in order to comprehend Buddhism. Actually, Japanese Buddhists read the sutras in Chinese and came to understand Buddhist thought in Chinese translation. After the thirteenth century, (the Kamakura period), attempts to understand Buddhism using Japanese texts were made, and in Tokugawa times there was also preaching in ordinary everyday language. However, the main terms were still technical terms of Chinese translation and the transfer to Japanese was not too successful. In the Meiji period, efforts began to clarify the definition of concepts by tracing back to the Indian root word, following the manner of research in Europe. One section of the scholarly world attempted to translate this to modern Japanese, but the practice is still not too general. Consequently, it is common to interpret Buddhist doctrine and faith within a framework of Chinese characters. There are also instances in which Chinese characters are used to express Japanese ideas; misunderstandings thus arise, and they have come to differ to some extent from the way they are used in China. However, when you come to Buddhist terms in Chinese translation, it is frequent that misunderstanding flourishes even more. Chinese translations put Indian terms into Chinese according to fixed rules.

It is frequent that one Indian word will have various meanings. The same word with different nuances and synonyms are numerous. To try to give these with one Chinese word is too unnatural. For instance the word *rūpa* has the basic meaning of external appearance (外観), color (色彩), form (形), illusion (幻影), beauty (美), character (性格), special quality (特質), type (種類), appearance (様式), but according to the way it is used, other meanings also appear. For instance *rūpa* applies to the material realm (物質, 肉体) as in the case when the structural elements of the phenomenal world are classified in Buddhism into five types (five *skandha*). The Indian term *rūpa* which had such a complicated connotation was always designated by (色) in Chinese character. It was not very easy at first to grasp the meaning of the root word from this one character. Despite the fact that we must distinguish generally about ten meanings in the one important Buddhist word *Dharma*, usually only one single Chinese character (法) is used. From the side of the characters, the problem becomes still more complicated by the fact that there are many implications from special nuances and from numerous ways of usage.

When the flavor of the Japanese method of using Chinese characters is added, it becomes still more troublesome. The Japanese never tried to translate the Buddhist Chinese into daily language (the same is true of Confucianism), or they could not. This fact indicates that on the side of the Japanese language there lacked a method of conception and expression in just adopting it. (After Meiji there was nothing to do but to rely on the difficult Chinese characters to translate Western European thought.)

It is said that thought form and language form have a close relation. In India, China and Japan the modes of expression completely vary and, consequently, the way of thinking differs somewhat. As in the case of philosophical thought, we can say the same thing for the content of faith. It is particularly conspicuous in usages of logical thought.

Indian logic developed from about the first or second century of the Western era, and after the fifth century excellent logicians appeared even in Buddhism. Hsüan Tsang (600–664 A.D.) introduced this logic called *Immyô* (*Hetuvidyā*) to China but the understanding of his disciples was extremely inadequate. We discover enormous errors in the commentaries which they wrote. This science of causes, *Immyô-gaku*, came to Japan along with the study of *Yuishiki* (Consciousness Only) thought. The tradition still continues to the present time in the so-called *Hossô* sect. There is a great quantity of commentaries. Since the understanding of basic points is lacking, misunderstanding is frequent. Indian logic has a structure which resembles greatly the formal logic which developed in Europe. Because the Indian language has a structure similar to that of Greek and Latin it is natural that their logical forms share resemblance. Chinese language could not be used in Indian style logic because the ending of words is not clear. It is not only a problem of language, but it is related to the differences in the character of thought. Since the Japanese learned Indian logic which had been misinterpreted in Chinese characters and further in Japanese letters, which differed completely from the Chinese as regards language and traditions of thought, the result has been nothing less than the vain rotation of thought. Though there are differences in degree, the same thing can be said concerning the reception of Buddhist metaphysics, ethics and religious thought in general. It is a fact that there were some Japanese who were successful to a certain degree in passing over such barriers to grasp the basic form of Buddhism. But the greater part of the Japanese, instead of aiming at an objective apprehension of foreign culture as such, desired more to select (from foreign culture), according to a subjective standard, only what was convenient for them. According to the result of contemporary comparative study in what are recognized as the distinctive characteristics of Japanese Buddhism, appear those which have been made with the knowledge the Japanese happened to have, being deficient in objective knowledge, rather than that they chose freely viewing from a broad perspective. What is called the advance or development of Buddhism is probably the convenience of man. We, who stand on the point of comparative study, cannot say at all that Japanese Buddhism, which has been transformed by misunderstanding and insufficient knowledge, is the essence of Buddhism.

Even though the understanding of Indian Buddhism is beside the point, to what extent at all have the Japanese been able to learn Chinese Buddhism?

We often hear the question: "Do the priests who read the sutras every day understand to any extent their contents?" We cannot answer this unqualifiedly, but, generally in Japanese Buddhist Orders, the sutras do not exist in order to be understood; their primary role is their use in ceremonies. We may say that the sutras were never given as a support for the faith of the general believer as the Bible for the Christian. Even in medieval Europe the general believer was prohibited from reading the Bible. It is only because there was no such desire to read, that there was no need to prohibit it in Japan.

The reading of the sutras, apart from ceremonial chanting by the priests, was extremely limited. For those who did enter into the content of the sutras in research it was nothing more than an addiction for playing with ideas within the framework set by the Sui and T'ang period commentators. Such questions as to what relation the concepts of the world and man had to our real existence were almost never treated. For instance, Mount Hiei was one center of Japanese Buddhism from the end of the eighth century, but we may note the fact that *Tendai* doctrine which was its most important study had no relation to human existence. (This fact may be compared to the real influence on medieval European society which Thomas Aquinas' theology exerted.)

It appears that Japanese Buddhists did not attempt strongly to translate the Buddhist sutras in Chinese translation into their own language, because they felt no real need for it, beside the fact that it was a task which exceeded their abilities. There was no necessity to have the ordinary priest or believer understand it. If one could read the Chinese text and grasp it for himself, that was sufficient.

However, the understanding of Chinese was limited to the point of grasping the meaning by running the eye over the Chinese text. The direct transmission of intention from mouth to ear, from man to man, was extremely rare. How many men were there among the many priests that went to T'ang and Sung China who could converse freely, or discuss, and ask questions of the Chinese about deep problems of religion and philosophy?

Even in the cases of Saichô and Kûkai, (they went together to T'ang China in 804), only Kûkai had linguistic ability to discuss freely. But Saichô departed in August with interpreters and arrived in China after fifty-four days. In May of the next year he left to return to Japan. Thus, he stayed in China exactly eight months. We cannot think that in this short time he could speak freely without interpreters. Moreover, the area which he visited was Chekiang in South China, where the language problem would be all the more difficult.

There are two priests from Japan who went to study in China and whose language abilities are reported in Chinese history. They are Chô-nen and Jakushô. Chônen entered Sung China in 982 and returned to Japan in 987. In the *Sung History* (*Sungshi*) it is recorded that: "Chônen can read books skillfully but cannot understand Chinese. If you inquire about Japanese ways, he answers by writing a sentence as follows." The same thing is recorded in the *Yuan History* (*Genshi*) also.

Even for Jakushô who went to Sung China in 1002 the statement appears in the *Sung History*:

> Jakushô does not understand Chinese but knows Chinese characters. He is very skillful in writing characters. He answers questions entirely by writing.

The *Yuan History* is generally the same. Jakushô stayed there and died in 1034, at the age of seventy-three. So it is quite possible that he mastered Chinese conversation later on.

Because Dôgen entered Sung China after first learning spoken Chinese, he does not appear to have been lacking in conversational ability. But when we observe that he studied with Ju-tsing of T'ien t'ung shan, and particularly when we see that he received permission to ask questions individually at any time as necessary, (*Hôkyôki* by Dôgen) he probably felt some handicap in conversing with his Chinese comrades.

Of course, each of the persons given here was skilled in reading Chinese. However, they were limited to the sphere of knowledge which is understood through seeing with the eye. We may suppose that there was more danger of falling into formalism than grasping the living thought. It is probable that the vital movement of words was lost when they were reduced to written text. In order to make up for that loss it is natural that some countermeasure must be devised. When one considers the influence that linguistic limitations exert on the understanding of thought, we must recognize that it was a considerable barrier in the importation of Chinese Buddhism into Japan.

Chinese Buddhist Priests in Japan

Though most of the Japanese Buddhist priests who went to China to study were lacking in conversational ability, what about the Chinese priests who visited Japan? We can inquire into the firmness of resolve of such as Chien-chen (Ganjin) who came to Japan in the Nara period (754) because he overcame frequent obstacles. Originally, however, they did not have the aim of propagating the religion confronting the common people directly, but aimed at performing rites to offer the precepts to specially designated men. It is said that Fa-tsin (Hosshin) who came to Japan along with Chien-chen was facile in Japanese, and propagated the religion in the Sanuki district in Shikoku, but we do not know the details.

During the Kamakura period there were many Chinese priests who came to Japan fleeing the upheavals at the end of the Southern Sung era, but it appears that they were not able to communicate their wishes sufficiently because of the language barrier and difference in thought pattern. Lan-chi Tao-lung (Rankei Dôryû) came to Japan in 1246 and succeeded in gaining the confidence of Hôjô Tokiyori. He was welcomed as the first generation in the establishment of Kenchôji temple in Kama-kura, but he suffered being often considered a spy.

Wu an Pu ning (Gottan Funei) who came to Japan in 1260 had a difficult time. After the death of Tokiyori in 1263, he incurred dis-pleasure and in that year returned home.

It was not very pleasant even for Yin-yüan who transmitted the *Ôbaku* school of the *Zen* sect in the Edo period. He arrived in Nagasaki in 1654, fleeing the troubles attending the end of the Ming and the beginning of the Ching dynasties. There was a clash between about twenty Chinese priests who accompanied Yin-yüan when he came to Nagasaki and some seventy Japanese priests, because they were not conversant in the Japa-nese language. Their customs and rites did not exactly correspond and it appears that both sides were discomfited. In displeasure they thought many times to return home, but finally they established Ôbakusan Manpukuji temple in Uji, a suburb of Kyoto. After that, there was no end to the slander which Japanese priests spoke of Yin-yüan.

There are many such examples beside these. While the Chinese priests were frequently handicapped in using Japanese, there was a tendency on the part of the Japanese not to become acquainted with the Chinese who differed in language and custom.

Of course, it happened that there was also frequent friction because of differences in language and customs among the Christians both in the 16th century and in Christianity after the Meiji restoration. Generally, however, the ordinary believer appears to have become more intimate with the foreign Christian teacher than in the case of Buddhism. This is worthy of note. In the case of Buddhism the Japanese, because of their preconceptions, probably had an excessive sense of difference toward the Chinese who resembled them in complexion.

The Japanese, more or less, have probably possessed this feeling in every case where they adopted Buddhism from China. It appears that there are frequent resemblances between Chinese and Japanese when they use the same letters. However, perplexity can clearly be sensed in the transfer of such a complicated cultural phenomenon as Buddhism in the cultural interchange between two people who differ basically in their way of thinking.

In this way, when we view the history of Buddhism in Japan over 1,400 years, despite the fact that new movements based on influences from the continent developed and took shape, it was rare that continental Buddhism was submissively adopted.

The Quest for Truth

Although the substance of Japanese Buddhism was based on Chinese Buddhism, it was always known that Buddhism was originally an Indian religion. However, it has only been in recent times that direct relations with India have been established. The name of Tenjiku (the old name of India) has often had an unrealistic echo (for instance the literature of the Heian court).

There do not seem to have been many examples of Indian priests coming to Japan. There was the rare instance of a so-called Baramon Sôjô (Brahman bishop), Bodhisena, who arrived in Dazaifu together with Tao-süan (Dôsen) of T'ang China in 738. He had gone to make a pilgrimage through the places sacred to Buddha in Mt. Wu tai shan in the Shansi district of China, but came to Japan at the suggestion of a Japanese who had gone to T'ang China. In Japan, he became intimate with Rôben and Gyôgi. He was honored by the court and in 752 was the leader in the rite, called "Opening of the Buddha's Eyes" (Kaigen), in connection with the enshrining of the Great Buddha of Todaiji temple. We can well imagine that he had high scholarship, but actually we know absolutely nothing of what kind of influence he had on the Japanese people.

Fu-ch'eh (Buttetsu) who came to Japan with Bodhisena was a man of the country of Rin'yû (An-nam or Indo-China), and it is said that he transmitted the music called Rin'yû-gaku. We may note significantly that this was a direct contact with the Indian sphere of culture.

The number of Japanese priests who studied in China, crossing the sea in a time when travel was inconvenient, was about five or six hundred. But it was very rare that any had the desire to study in India.

In this sense, Shinnyo Hoshinnô (Priestly Imperial Prince), that is, Takaokashinnô, was unprecedented. The Prince was the third son of Emperor Heijô, and when Emperor Saga ascended the throne in 809, he became Crown Prince. The next year he was engulfed in the *Kusuko* disturbance. Retiring from the rank of Crown Prince, he entered a monastery in Tôdaiji. After he studied the doctrines of *Hossô* and *Sanron*, he learned the esoteric (*Mikkyô*) doctrines from Kûkai and became a very important figure in the *Shingon* sect. But, not being satisfied, he went to T'ang China in 861. Later, in 864, he went on a journey to India. From the region of Chukiang he traversed the mountain area of Yünnan and entered Malay where his letters stop. It is reported that he was eaten by a tiger in the same region. He was then seventy years old. There are few examples of such a vigorous intellectual appetite.

In the Kamakura period Eisai, who is regarded as the founder of the *Rinzai* sect in Japan, attempted to travel to India. The first time Eisai went to Sung China and stayed there only about five or six months (1168). After returning to Japan he resolved that there was nothing else to do but go to India, in order to complete a penetrating study of Buddhism. In 1187 he again crossed over to Sung China and sought permission to travel to India. But at that time Sung power did not extend to North China, then under the control of the Chin (Tartars) and the Si-Hsia (Tanguts). The road to the West was closed. Because he could not get permission to go by the South Sea route, he had to give up hope of going to India.

It was Myôe Shônin Kôben of Toganoo, who attempted the journey after Eisai. At about the time new sects were being established, Kôben revived the old *Kegon* tradition. From his childhood he had purposed to travel to India. Many times he planned it.

Around 1203–1205 he studied the travel diaries of Hsüen-tsang for that purpose, and made notes and plans. He determined the distance from Chang An in China to Rājagriha in Central India as 50,000 *li*, in Japanese measure 8,333 *ri* and 12 *chô*. If he were to leave Chang An on New Year's Day and travel eight *ri* a day, he would arrive in Rājagriha in the third year on October 10th. If he did seven *ri* in one day, he would arrive in the fourth year on February 20th. With a pace of five *ri* per day he would arrive on June 10th of the sixth year. However, due to illness, he finally had to abandon his plans. After that conditions in Japan and Asia made it impossible to attempt to travel to India. Early in Meiji, Shimaji Mokurai made a pilgrimage to the Buddhist monuments in India on the way to Europe (1872–1873). Later great priests and scholars of every sect following this example increased in number. It is recent in our memories that many Japanese Buddhist followers visited India for the rites commemorating the 2,500th year of Buddha's Nirvana in 1956 as well as on other occasions.

As I related previously, materials for the study of Buddhism in Japan were generally in Chinese. Since even in Chinese Buddhism, which was the womb of Japanese Buddhism, there was never any study of the Indian language apart from the translators, it is natural that means and materials were lacking for the study of the original text for the Japanese.

It is certain that a very great number of Sanskrit texts were brought to China, but they have never been discovered outside the remote regions. Among the literature which was imported to Japan from China, the number of Sanskrit texts was never large. Because they were preserved as treasures, the ancient documents exist now. The Sanskrit texts of *baiyô* (a paper of dried leaves used for writing and copying), which had been transmitted to Hôryûji by the Imperial House, had belonged orig-inally to the *Zen* priests, Nan-yüeh and Nien-shan, according to a tem-ple tradition. In the 16th year of Suiko Tennô (608) Onono-Imoko-brought them to Japan. Whether we can believe this tradition is a ques-tion, but according to the expert opinion of modern specialists (Bühler and others), it is recognized, from a consideration of the style, as an item from that period. It is certain that the Sanskrit script is related to that used widely in North India from the eighth century to the tenth. Perhaps it was transmitted from Central Asia to China from the seventh to the eighth century.

In Japan the style of writing Sanskrit or grammar was called *Shittan* This comes from the Sanskrit term *Siddha* which means complete (*Jôju*) or favorable omen (*Kisshô*). It may be considered a word which denotes the symbols of the alphabet. We call the symbols of the letters *matataimon*. However, at the beginning of the 11th century, an Arabian, Al Biruni, introduced the style of character as the *Siddha-mātrikā* which was used widely at the time in North India from Kashmir to Benares. The Sanskrit writing preserved in our country can be considered to be of the same lineage.

Apart from Hôryûji there were texts of old *baiyô* paper which were imported before the Nara period in five or six temples such as the Kôkiji temple. There was an interest in Sanskrit in the Nara court, but in the Heian period, it became at least a necessity to study Sanskrit with the establishment of the two sects of *Tendai* and *Shingon* by Saichô and Kûkai. In the esoteric *Mikkyô* teaching, along with the Chinese texts, spells in Sanskrit writing and language were used independently. Moreover, a special science, called *Shittan-gaku*, was created, the tradition of which has been transmitted to the modern age with some modification.

Beginning with Kûkai, monks who went to T'ang China at the beginning of the Heian period frequently learned Sanskrit there, and they returned with books of *baiyô* paper and ordinary paper. We may note among the scholars of this era Annen (end of ninth century) who wrote the eight volume *Shittanzô* (Sanskrit glossary). The fifty-sound syllabary pattern of the a, i, u, e, o which is used even now in Japanese, was an imitation of the order of letters in Sanskrit, and they are considered to be from the hand of Annen's school.

Since the Kamakura period, the Sanskrit tradition had been preserved in the *Shingon* school, but after the Edo period it became a real subject of study. The pioneer was Jôgon who established Reiunji temple in Yushima in Edo. He studied and copied the *baiyô* texts of Hôryûji and wrote the four-volume *Kabontaihon* (*Comparative Translation of Chinese and Sanskrit*) and the eight-volume, *Shittan Sanmitsushô* (*Three Original Sanskrit Texts*) besides others. Keichû who studied Sanskrit under Jôgon deserves special note from the point of view of the history of Sanskrit study in Japan and also for epochal achievements in the study of Japanese. Even the nationalist Motoori Norinaga saw the importance of the influence of Sanskrit study on the national language.

After Jôgon, the teacher and pupil, Donjaku and Jakugon, studied Sanskrit, but it was Jiun Sonja Onkô who left behind the most excellent achievements. Onkô also belonged to the *Shingon* school but he advocated *Shôbôritsu* (Precept of the True *Dharma*), and he is said to have been a monk with both scholarship and virtue. He opened new ground in unprecedented areas in the study of Sanskrit. He studied such books as the *Fugengyôgansan* (*Bhadra-cāri*), *Han'nyashingyô* (*Prajñāpāramitāhrdaya*) and *Amidakyô* (*Sukhāvatī-vyūha*), which were copies of Sanskrit texts transmitted long ago. He not only understood the meaning of the vocabulary, but he studied inductively the change of verb endings together with nouns, adjectives and numbers single handedly. He determined the rules of grammar, and consequently even tried to retranslate *Han'nyarishukyô* from Chinese to Sanskrit. His Sanskrit study is preserved in the Kôkiji temple just as it was in the 1,000-volume *Bongakushinryô* (*Encyclopedic Dictionary of Sanskrit*). Only a portion of it has been published, but its result is worthy of admiration. It was about 1759–1771 that Onkô concentrated his efforts on the study of Sanskrit. At that time only very few men in Europe had an interest in Sanskrit. Because it was earlier than the year (1785) when the Englishman Wilkins translated the *Bhagavad Gītā*, we can say Onkô stole the march in that study. Onkô taught Sanskrit also to his disciples, but it is a shame that no one with the ability to take it up after him appeared.

Therefore, it came about that Japanese learned Sanskrit from Europe after Meiji. That Onkô, only one seeing man among a thousand blind men, should have performed such service is something worthy of a Japanese. We must express admiration for the quiet efforts of the men who preserved the ancient tradition until Onkô. The greater part of the Buddhists were satisfied with parroting Chinese Buddhism and adapting it, but we may say that it speaks well of a particular aspect of Japanese Buddhism that there were people who continued such serious efforts.

There appears to have been one ideal running through all the Japanese priests who attempted to travel to India and learn Sanskrit. They desired to know the nature of Buddhist truth and tried to practice it. They were not satisfied with only the Chinese sutras given casually and the teaching of the Chinese. They deeply aspired to seek out the more fundamental shape of Buddhism. There lay across their path great obstacles such as we cannot imagine looking at it from today. No difficulty at all could break their spirit of seeking the true *Dharma*.

The inner demand of desiring to realize the original form of Buddhism naturally became a search for the true teaching of Śākyamuni. The men who had such aspirations believed that the first requirement was to practice the correct discipline (*kairitsu*).

A Buddhism with no discipline is impossible. Whoever does not guard the discipline just as Śākyamuni taught it has not the qualifications to be a Buddhist monk. This was the basic view which these men held in common. All the men we have mentioned in the previous two sections, who attempted the journey to India, studied Sanskrit, and each stressed the importance of the precepts. It is simply impossible to conceive of a monk in India or in China making light of the discipline. After Buddhism was transmitted to Japan also, thinking men always considered the preservation of the precepts as the life of Buddhism.

However it was by no means easy to practice the way of life of the precepts in Japan. It was a real problem. From early times a tendency to crafty wisdom was practiced comprised to a certain point with various excuses. These men who tried to restore fundamental Buddhism always took up the problem of discipline first. The following words appear in the writing of Dôgen who also sought fundamental Buddhism:

> One asks, "Should the man who chiefly practices *Zazen* keep the precepts?" He answers: "Keeping the discipline and precepts are, in other words, the rules of the *Zen* school and the traditions of the Buddha."

As is clear in the words of Dôgen, the discipline is considered the necessary requisite of *Zen* meditation for the unification of the spirit. This is not just the casual idea of Dôgen alone. It is taught repeatedly even in the sutras of original Buddhism.

Similarly in the Kamakura period Eizon valued the discipline. He entered the monastery at the age of 11 and studied esoteric teaching

(*Mikkyô*), practiced *Zen*, and was endowed with scholarship and virtue. Even though he was proficient in mental concentration (*Samādhi*) and wisdom (*Prajñā*) and had studied the exoteric and esoteric doctrines of Buddhism, he felt strongly that if this was not accompanied by the practice of the discipline, it came to nothing. Because tendencies were very strong which threw the discipline generally into confusion at that time, Eizon endeavored to disseminate the correct discipline and to restore the ancient rites as a result of studying the texts and his predecessors.

Later in the Edo period, we may note that Jôgon and Onkô of the *Shingon* school who were previously introduced as Sanskrit scholars, at the same time made positive efforts to restore the precepts. These men did not study merely to satisfy their curiosity or intellectual appetite, but they made serious efforts to practice essential Buddhism with their whole heart. The following words are transmitted as the work of Onkô and illustrate this:

> Once you bravely abandon home and enter the path with great pains, you must attain to the status of *Buddha*, being furnished with the knowledge of *Buddha*, preserving the discipline of *Buddha*, wearing the robe of *Buddha*, and doing the acts of *Buddha*. Stop imitating the teachers of the latter age, but live a pure life, do not drink spoiled milk mixed with water.

Moreover, it was also Onkô who noted that the way of making the *kesa* (Buddhist stole) since the T'ang era was erroneous. He taught and spread in the world the correct way of making the *kesa* based on the ancient sutra. We may say this reveals a critical spirit which tried to restore orthodox Buddhism according to accurate materials.

Then, what was the attitude of those who, yearning for India, studied Sanskrit and, emphasizing strict discipline, established fundamental Buddhism, toward the common people? Those who don't really know may imagine that such priests had an indifferent attitude being only interested in selfishly transcending the world. However, exactly the opposite is true. Actually, without exception, almost all of these men emphasized a fundamental and strict Buddhism. They approached the common people, and they were men who sought an increase in benefits for the common man. Let us look at two or three examples.

One of them is Dôshô who first transmitted a basic Buddhism after studying in T'ang China. In the year 661 he returned to Japan. He lectured on the *Yuishiki* (Consciousness-Only) doctrine and practiced *Zen* meditation (*Zazen*). According to his request, he had his body cremated. This was the first time cremation had been practiced in Japan. Cremation was a characteristic of Buddhism. Together with Buddhism, it was transmitted to China from India. It is natural that the Chinese, who considered the dead body important, were not pleased with this practice. Actually, even Hsüan Tsang, who was Dôshô's teacher, was buried humbly. Because there was no custom of cremation even in Japan, we can consider that Dôshô's request was true to the tradition of Buddhism. During his life he practiced *Zazen* and established a meditation hall in the southeast area of Gangôji temple. Dôshô traveled in various parts of the country over a period of about fifteen or sixteen years. He dug wells by the side of the road, and he provided ferries to cross the rivers. He also built bridges. It is said that it was Dôshô who constructed the first bridge over the Uji River (according to the tablet of the memorial at Ujibashi, the first man to make the bridge was Dôtô). We may count him as an example of an individual who was effective in social activity while pursuing high inner ideals and deeply immersed in *Zazen*.

We can take note of Gyôgi following Dôshô. Gyôgi also learned *Yuishiki* doctrine. Going into the mountain forests he practiced *Zazen*. When he traveled in various parts, those who followed wherever he went often numbered in the thousands. When people heard that Gyôgi was coming, they all gathered and reverenced him. He made bridges in places that were necessary for traffic, and he constructed dykes along the rivers. Whether young or old, every one came to help in his work, and the work gradually progressed. Wherever he lived, he planted fruit trees, and he built *dôjô* (seminaries for Buddhist priests) in forty-nine places. His popularity among the people knew no limits, and the government which felt some anxiety about his activity in 717 prohibited the religious activities of Gyôgi and his disciples. But in 743 he was welcomed by the court, and came to be valued as the chief person in the movement to construct the Great Buddha in Tôdaiji temple. Gyôgi also is an example of a man who harmonized social activity and inner depth.

In the Heian era there are also many examples of Buddhist priests who made projects of building bridges, supplying ferryboats, digging wells, and planting trees. Saichô also employed his mind for this, but Kûkai demonstrated his ability in frequent social projects such as the construction of reservoirs (Mannôike) in Sanuki, and the construction and administration of facilities for the education of poor youth (*Shugeishuchiin*).

In the Kamakura period also those who extended their hands positively for the sake of increasing the welfare of the common people generally valued the precepts highly. They were priests who practiced meditation.

What we call the *Zen* sect in later times comprised both the *Rinzai* school and the *Sôtô* school, and they were established in the Kamakura period. But in fact we may say that wherever there is Buddhism, there is surely *Zen*, and the actual practice of *Zen*, as we related above, is always connected to the practice of compassionate mercy and love. The following story is related by Dôgen about Eisai, the founder of the *Rinzai* school in Japan.

> When the late Abbot lived in Kenninji a lone poor man visited him. He said, "My family is destitute and we have food only for five or six days. My wife and child, the three of us, will starve to death. Please have mercy and save us." At that time there was no clothing, food or property in the room at all. When Eisai thought it over he had no plan. At that time, there was a little copper which he had beaten for the halo in order to make a figure of *Yakushi*. Taking this he folded it into a lump and gave it to the poor visitor. "With this you can escape starvation by exchanging it for food." The man was overjoyed and withdrew from his presence. Then his disciples said critically, "Certainly this is the halo of a Buddhist image, and you have given it to a common man. Isn't it a sin to use the things of Buddha as you wish?" The Abbot replied: "That is true, but, when I think of the Buddha's intention, he gave his body to all beings, dividing body, hands and feet. We must follow the Buddha's intention, even if we give the whole body of a Buddha to beings who may starve to death." Further he said: "Even though I may fall into evil paths by

this sin I just must keep beings from starving." (*Shôbôgenzô-zuimonki* no. 2.)

And Dôgen adds to this: "Those who are practicing now must consider the thought of our predecessors and be careful not to forget it."

Eizon, who made a great contribution in the practice of the precepts and their dissemination in the Kamakura period, moreover, at the same time, was a person who undertook great social projects. One of the outstanding of Eizon's projects was the salvation of the lower classes. The *Hinin* were the despised people (*senmin*), and they were segregated from society in general. They were either beggars or followed special, mean occupations. They also included lepers and those who were regarded as outside the sphere of society. Eizon often gave them money and rice. He repaired the dwellings of the lowly and the huts of the lepers. Besides this, he conferred the precepts on a great number of the outcasts, so that they would not cause trouble among the population. Further, it is said that he offered food for fifty or sixty thousand starving people in the year 1268. This was all done from the spontaneous gifts of believers.

Ryôkanbô Ninshô, who was a disciple of Eizon, went so far as to vow to stop eating meat at the age of thirteen. He was very diligent in the study and practice of the precepts but made achievements in social projects which excelled his teacher. At the time of the famine of 1274 and the plagues of dysentery of 1283, he carried on great activity with the help of his disciples. The sphere of his work was very broad including such things as: rescue of beggars, administration of hospitals, and care of orphans. If we make a general accounting of his life, the construction of eighty-three temples, one hundred eighty-nine bridges, seventy-one roads, and thirty-three wells can be enumerated. Besides these, he built public baths, hospitals and inns for beggars. He provided *Hiden-in* (Field of Pity Hall, a place to care for people in distress) and *Kyôden-in* (the main sanctuary) in Shitennôji to commemorate the achievement of Shôtoku Taishi. In the Kuwadani hospital, established in 1287, in the space of twenty years there were 46,800 fully cured persons, and 10,450 dead persons. Up to eighty per cent were helped. It probably required extraordinary efforts to attain such good results. When he was in Sai-daiji temple at Nara, he restored the leper hospital at Kitayama Han-nyazaka in which Empress Kômyô is said to have washed leper patients. Every other day in the morning he carried to town a crippled patient who could not go out to beg and carried him back to the hospital in the evening. And thus the man was enabled to live by begging. This con-tinued for several years without interruption.

It must be especially added that Ninshô established a hospital for horses in 1298. This was also based on unlimited compassion toward living beings.

In the original Indian Buddhism as we see also in King Asoka, the spirit of compassion and its realization are emphasized. It is not only true in Buddhism, but it is also true in Jainism. The believers in this religion at present provide hospitals for animals and old age homes, to say nothing of their social service. Unconsciously Ninshô took the same course.

From the Kamakura to the Muromachi period there were many social projects such as charity, and public works carried out by priests. When we come to the Edo period, there was much less social work done by priests. This can probably be accounted for by the fact that the institu-tions of the Shôgunate and the clans were much improved, but Buddhism became spiritless.

In the Edo period there is the case of Dôkô Tetsugen who is a com-paratively outstanding example. It is noted that he was a *Zen* priest of the *Ôbaku* sect who learned from the Chinese priest Yin yüan. The reason is that Yin yüan was one who gave fresh spirit to Japanese Bud-dhism which had shrunk completely under the religious policy of the Shôgunate.

Because of that there also arose friction between him and Japanese priests. It is due to the influence of Yin yüan that Tetsugen, his disciple, was extraordinarily active at that time.

Tetsugen was born in a branch temple of the Honganji in the province of Higo. At the age of thirteen he was ordained and was a married *Shin* sect priest. He lamented that the priests of the sect were ranked higher according to the standing of their temple even though they were without virtue or ability. At twenty-six years of age he went to Nagasaki and met Yin yüan. He became the disciple of Yin yüan's successor, Muan Chengtao. His name is eternal because he accomplished the great undertaking of printing the *Daizôkyô* (Tripitaka Buddhist Canon). His works of mercy were innumerable such as giving clothes and food to the poor, providing medicine for the sick, caring for orphans and asking for clemency for prisoners.

On the occasion of a great famine in Western Japan in the spring of 1682, he gathered many refugees in Zuiryûji temple (Tetsugenji) in Ôsaka and gave them money and rice. He emptied all the provisions stored in the temple, but they were not sufficient. In a letter requesting from Yamazaki Hansaiemon of Edo a loan of money for charity, there is a passage dated February 22nd.

> I started this work on the 13th of this month. Because all other persons stopped giving charity, the beggars are having a very hard time. Because I am doing charity work, it is a great help to them. On the 13th, 2,000 persons, on the 14th, 6,000 and from the 15th on more than 10,000 were helped. Recently more than 20,000 were helped. Such being the case, I am not able to provide for such great need. If I stop giving charity, all will surely die. Therefore, I wouldn't stop giving even if I had to sell my temple or cut off my fingers (for food).

According to his biography, his charity work lasted over a month averaging more than 10,000 persons a day. This, indeed, was a great rescue work.

We must note that in the case of Tetsugen, the practice of meditation, the pursuit of Buddhist truth and the public welfare were united into one.

I do not mean to say that I have included all the representative priestly social workers with only those whom I have given above. Besides these, there are many known and unknown persons who carried out such practices. For example, there was Shunjôbô Chôgen, who learned Pure Land teaching from Hônen, and did many social works besides the re-construction of Tôdaiji. We must mention especially Kûya in the tenth century and Ippen in the thirteenth century. Those traveling priests who succeeded Ippen also belong to this group. In short, they were persons who entered and lived among the people and were called "holy persons" or "saints" (*shônin*). Traveling about the country, they built roads, bridges, repaired buildings. planned irrigation and rescued refugees. Their achievements were truly great.

From what I have stated, we can see that generally there are two types of Buddhist social workers. The first is the Buddhist priest, proper, so to speak, who pursues profound Buddhist truth, theoretically and practically, ever aspiring for the highest ideal and their own spiritual elevation. The second are the holy persons and saints who abandon their own desires, negating themselves completely, and merge their lives with the people. Those who belong to the latter are worthy of respect, but I should specially like to discuss the former here. The reason is that people do not doubt that those who negate themselves and live with the people should devote themselves to the benefit of the public. However, some people may think that those who search for the highest ideal in their own emancipation may forget the existence of the others. Such misunderstanding exists even among those who study the history of Japanese Buddhism. Therefore, I explained at length quoting many examples.

It is quite natural from the fundamental standpoint of Buddhism that aspirants for the high ideal of Buddhism should strive for the welfare of people and broadly speaking, all living beings. The principles of "perfection of (the aim of) benefiting self and others" or the ideal of "aspiring upward for enlightenment (*Bodhi*) and saving sentient beings downward," are time-honored. They can be seen clearly in Śākyamuni's own life and in the achievements of his successors. All the Buddhist teachings and theories, as well as practical morals, are centered on the one point; that is, the perfection of the ideal in one's self and others. Unfortunately in East Asia a secondary, additional element, that is, religious ceremony or ideological playing with doctrine, came to the fore in Buddhism. Therefore, as a result, the original practicality of Buddhism was lost sight of. But, when we try to grasp the original form of Buddhism by means of scholarly research and practice, there naturally is the consciousness of lofty ideals as well as boundless compassion toward the common man which is realized in action.

Hence it is said, "The Buddha immersed in mental concentration (*Samādhi*) is the more fundamental form and the Buddha, when active in saving men, must all the more turn to the *Samādhi*-Buddha, the more he is active." (Susumu Yamaguchi).

Here we will quote what Arnold Toynbee says about Christianity on this problem:

> Actually, it would appear easy to prove that religious persons were useful in the concrete requirements of society. If we consider as examples such men as St. Francis of Assisi, St. Vincent de Paul, John Wesley, and David Livingston, it may be said that there is no need for demonstration. Therefore, we will cite as examples here persons who were either commonly viewed as exceptional people, or subjected to ridicule. These people were said to be both "God-intoxicated" and "anti-social." It was also a joke that they were saints, and they were ridiculed by cynical men who called them "good men" in the worst sense. This was precisely the case with St. Anthony of the desert and St. Stylites. It is clear that these saints remained in the "world," and on account of their being separated from companions, it turned out that they had a much more active relationship with many more people than, on the contrary, they would, if they had spent their lives at a specific job. The retired saint ruled the world more effectively than the Emperor in the capital. The reason is that the pursuit of spiritual nature on the part of these individuals by seeking spiritual intercourse with God, as a social form, moved people more powerfully than any kind of secular social service on the political level.

If we mean by the first type those who acted socially, putting into practice profound scholarship and high religious experience, there is also the second type of men who similarly seek the truth in study and practice and, while possessing it, they transcend such scholarship immersing themselves in a pure and simple life. They exhibited unlimited compassion for all living beings and all men and lived with common men. In many cases such persons were not known because they were reluctant to speak about themselves. Here I'll give Tôsui and Ryôkan as examples. Each rejected scholarship and fame completely and mingled with the people. Turning against artificial civilization, they led life with nature as their friend. Their attitude probably seems negative, but it hides within a strong resolve. Externally they led a clear and pure existence and had great influence on many people.

Tôsui Unkei was a *Zen* priest born at Yanagawa in Chikugo province in the seventeenth century. At the age of seven he entered a monastery in Hizen. He fasted and meditated under the sky. He liked to dwell in the mountains and to do *Zazen* on the riverside. When he was twenty he stayed in Kichijôji temple in Edo and mingled with such famous priests as Takuan. He met Yin-yüan in Nagasaki and, as a pupil of Yin-yüan he mingled intimately with Mu-an (Mokuan) and Kao-tsüan (Kôsen) who came from Ming China. He became head of Hôgonji temple in Higo and Zenrinji temple in Hizen, but every day he went out with his begging bowl and sought food for himself. Any remainder of food he gave to beggars. Many priests and men and women believers gathered, admiring his virtue. One day without warning he left his temple, and lost his way. His disciples organized search parties, but he lived by begging his way to Kyoto, Ôtsu and Ise with other beggars. Sometimes he made straw sandals and sold them. A disciple named Jinshû met Tôsui begging in the Higashiyama area of Kyoto. "Please let me accompany you" he requested and followed after Tôsui. On a side street they saw a beggar who had died. They buried him and Tôsui, taking his begging bowl, ate the remaining food with relish. The disciple tried to imitate him but the food only got as far as his mouth. When Tôsui saw this he said, "It is too difficult for you. Let us part." What the pupil heard at the time was a poem composed by Tôsui.

> If I live this way I am free and at ease. Even if I wear ragged clothes or have a broken bowl, I am very leisurely.
> If I get hungry, I eat; If I get thirsty, I drink. Whether the world says it is good or bad, I care not.

Because Christians were prosecuted after that time, people who thought it was a pity that suspicions were raised about Tôsui, the beggar, gave him an *Amitābha* image of Ôtsue painting. Tôsui hung it in his hut as he was told, but he noted with charcoal cinders:

> Even though it is a small house, I will give you lodging, O, *Amida*. Don't think that I take refuge in you!

Even if it appears that Tôsui compromised with the world, it is proof that he had backbone. Because a believer gave him a great amount of rice with the excuse that it was leftover food, Tôsui spent his latter days selling vinegar made from the rice in Takagamine in the north of Kyoto calling himself Suyadôzen or Tsûnen. He died here at the age of more than seventy years.

If we speak from the consensus of Buddhist monks in Japan, Tôsui's case appears unexampled. But it was the usual path for monks in Śākyamuni's fellowships to live by begging. The life of begging is naturally humbling. One cannot say he likes or dislikes the food. These two points are aspects of the ideal monk's existence. In later generations a common existence in a monastery appeared even in India, but the consciousness that traveling about and begging were true principles was not altered.

Ryôkan was born as the eldest son of a village leader of Izumozaki in Echigo. In his youth he studied Chinese classics. At sixteen, in order to follow the steps of his father, he became an apprentice of the village head, but at the age of eighteen he gave the house over to his younger brother and entered the Kôshôji temple of the *Sôtô* sect in the next town. He was called Ryôkan or Daigu. At twenty-two he went to Entsûji temple in Bitchû. Here he received strict training as a *Zen* priest. During that period also he traveled in Chûgoku, Kyûshû, and Shikoku. When he heard of his father's suicide twenty years later, he went to Kyoto and took a seat in the memorial service. He set foot in his native village and only stood before the gate of his birthplace. Then immediately he set forth roaming about. He spent his life begging at hermitages and old temples one after the other with Izumozaki as his center. For about fifteen or sixteen years after his forty-eighth year, the period of his full maturity, he lived in the Gogôan in Kugamisan. From about his sixtieth year, he had a hermitage in the compound of Otogo shrine at the foot of Mount Kugami. At seventy years he lived in a hut in the villa of a believer, and died at seventy-five, while receiving warm care from those people. His farewell to the world reads:

What may I leave as my memorial?

Flowers in Spring, Cuckoos in Summer, and Maple leaves in Autumn!

We know nothing of Ryôkan's period as a novitiate or of his time of travels because he said nothing about himself. He bent his whole energy to strong effort and practice. It appears he had not even time to worry about food or clothes. His life, polished by many years of practice, may be likened to a gem. Because he was without desire, he was not obstructed by worldly affairs, and he was completely merged with nature. Peculiar as his conduct looked, it was nothing but the manifestation of a lofty personality. Even now Ryôkan's poems and writings are highly valued. He was not only an artist, but exhibited the ultimate in the perfection of humanity.

What we admire most in Ryôkan was his unlimited love for men, animals, plants, in fact, all nature. He is reputed to have said:

I must have sympathy for living beings, even to birds and beasts.

He was happy to give his leftover food to birds and animals. He put lice in his pocket and let mosquitos draw from his legs. In order to let a bamboo shoot grow, he cut his floor and tore open his roof. This was very natural for Ryôkan.

But he never forgot to love mankind. He loved beggars; gave to robbers; loved farmers; and played with the children and the innocent. We may call him a person who attained the sphere of egolessness which is realized through the absence of desire. The coarseness of his food and clothing was surprising, but in his hermitage he had only one earthenware mortar. He ground *miso*, polished rice, and washed his hands with it. He brings to mind the Greek philosopher Diogenes.

There are very many famous anecdotes told of him, but what we wanted to call attention to especially here was the fact that his lofty attitude has the discipline of *Zen* as its presupposition. Naturally it is in harmony with the spirit of original Buddhist discipline. Actually, Ryôkan was one of a small number whom we are not ashamed to call disciples of Śākyamuni. However, he never fell into self-righteous self-satisfaction. We must call him a fundamental Buddhist on the two points that he gave his whole self in the service of others, and that he led men broadly transcending sectarian distinctions. As we might expect, Ryô-kan's influence has been broad and deep even till today. When one exhibits the Buddhist life in his existence he experiences it in himself first, and then individual and social existence becomes brighter.

Compassion and Tolerance

Within the stream of Japanese Buddhism we have sought the original nature of Buddhism, and we mentioned some priests whom we may call representatives of fundamental Buddhism not only in individual theory and practice, but also in their actions toward society. But we must recognize that within Japanese Buddhism, apart from these persons, there was by comparison an overwhelmingly large number of unorthodox sects. In a word, because these unorthodox persons lacked the desire or the ability to seek the fundamental nature of Buddhism in an objective historical foundation, they misunderstood what was given by chance as the fundamental thing. They mistakenly affirmed that "this is Buddhism" from a subjective judgment. Of course, we cannot conclude, from the Buddhist standpoint, that it is generally impossible to attain a high religious experience by activities having these misinterpretations as a kind of agent and also by a purification of life.

It is said that Buddha's compassion is unlimited. The Buddha never taught specific, blessed men alone. The Buddha had the meek and indigent as companions. As it was with the historical person Śākyamuni, so the Buddha who has taken various forms as an object of faith, is said to have a fundamental nature of wisdom and compassion. Consequently, all beings are the objects of salvation. Hence, Buddhism, which is originally a religion of emancipation, is at the same time a religion of salvation. This tendency can be seen even in the earliest Buddhist Order, and through the ages various forms of salvation have been added to it.

In connection with compassion, there is the Buddhist characteristic of tolerance. Religions such as monotheism call those teachings which differ either paganism or evil teachings, and there is a tendency to hate them as they hate evil spirits. However, Buddhism does not force a particular doctrine on men. It causes each person to awaken the latent *Bodhi*-mind within him. It has the aim to lead one to the perfection of his humanity. Therefore, even though one has different views and beliefs, they are not completely rejected. On the contrary, it vitalizes the convictions and the religious experience the individual already possesses, and enables him to reach the highest level. Therefore the forms of faith which appear at first sight to be superstition, particularly those of family or race, are not attacked frontally. Rather, the way is taken to bring about progress to a higher religious experience using these beliefs as a media.

Compassion and tolerance are certainly ideal attitudes in religion, but evils have also accompanied them on occasion. It has even come about that the original nature of Buddhism has been lost by the affirmation of a vulgar form of faith. It has been frequent that the economic law that bad money drives out good applies also to the history of religion.

Even so, the compromises in India or the Indian cultural sphere were limited. While the elements of the regional popular faiths were stronger, they were corrected by theoretical and practical reflection, or they were given a new interpretation. That limitation lay in the fundamental concept which we call the *Bodhi*-mind.

It is natural when we consider religions of salvation that the concept of *Tariki* (literally other-power), should appear.

This is the concept that man is saved by the compassion of an existence apart from man such as a Buddha or a Bodhisattva, rather than by pursuit of an ideal self through one's own striving (*Jiriki* or self-power). But *Tariki* salvation is never ultimate according to real Indian literature. For instance, we cannot say that being born in the Pure Land by faith is the attainment of the ultimate ideal. It can only be said that the attainment of the *Bodhi*-mind is easier in the Pure Land than in this present world. There is no difference even in Pure Land faith itself that the ultimate aim is the perfection of *Bodhi*.

However, in China it was connected to a different concept of the after-life. The concept appeared in which birth in the Pure Land itself became the ultimate human ideal. This idea came to Japan and was further simplified. The three aspects of biological death, birth in the Pure

Land, and becoming Buddha were confused. This goal was to be realized by rites carried out by Buddhist priests. Japanese Buddhism degenerated to the point where the dead person was called *Hotoke* (Buddha), and they prayed to Buddha for the happiness of the dead by sutra recitation or the *Nembutsu*, that is, repetition of the expression "Adoration to the Buddha of Infinite Life and Light." This was accepted without question. The fundamental ideal of Buddhism in pursuing the realization of human ideals was changed to rites for dead spirits.

Of course, it is true that there were psychological and social bases in each stage of these changes, and the possibility was contained in the Buddhist attitude of extreme compassion and tolerance, which permitted the development of substitutes for the real thing. As the result of excessive divergence, there appeared sects which varied considerably from fundamental Buddhism. Besides the Buddhist attitude of tolerance the new concept of the Last Age of the *Dharma* (*Mappô*) also made it possible for such abnormal sects to appear.

The Last Age of the *Dharma* is contrasted with the age of the Right *Dharma* (*Shôbô*). Right *Dharma* means Buddha's true teaching. It signified originally that the words which the Buddha taught would last one thousand years as they had been taught. There was also a theory that thought the Buddha's words would last more than one thousand years; people would only practice this teaching effectively for the first thousand years (*Abhidharma Kośa*).

This concept leads to the idea that after the age of the Right *Dharma*, the Counterfeit *Dharma* (*Zôhô*) would appear as its substitute (Counterfeit *Dharma* is that teaching which resembles but is not the correct *Dharma*). The Last Age of the *Dharma* comes after the disappearance of the Counterfeit *Dharma*. ("Disappearance of the *Dharma*" if we make a direct translation of the original term *Mappô*.) The concept of the Last Age was taught in India, but it became especially popular in China about the middle of the sixth century. This was a pessimistic view stirred up by unrest in individual existence caused by social commotion.

Such phenomenon is not limited to the East. In Rome toward the end of the first century, when society was in turmoil, John's *Apocalypse* was

composed in which the termination of the world and the creation of a
new world are described:

> An angel . . . seized the dragon . . . who is the devil and Satan and
> bound him for a thousand years, and threw him into the pit . . . that he
> deceive the nations no more, till the thousand years were ended. And
> when the thousand years are ended, Satan will be loosed from his prison
> and will come out to deceive the nations which are at the four corners of
> the earth, that is, Gog and Magog, to gather them for battle; . . .
> (Chapter 20).

The Christian eschatology is distinguished from the Chinese Buddhist
concept of the Last Age in many respects. But there is some resemblance
between the two in that the concept appeared at the time of social commotion and loss of individual self-confidence and also in that the period
lasts one thousand years.

It is also said that in Europe there was a fear that the world would
perish a thousand years after Christ. It is not a problem of the length of
the thousand years of time, but a fear reflecting contemporary social and
political unrest.

There was a similar circumstance in the popularity of the Chinese concept of the Last Age about the middle of the sixth century. Toward the
end of the North and South Dynasties, both dynasties underwent quick
changes of ruling authority which caused unrest among the people.
Confronting such anxiety among the people, it was, of course, the priests
who began to teach the idea of the Last Age as the cause of the world's
turmoil. I must repeat that social and individual insecurity and the concept of the Last Age were originally separate. It was the religionists who
explained this phenomenon by combining the two. Once these two
ideas were bound together, they gave rise to a certain common social
consciousness which stirred the people's mind like an invisible monster.

The concept of the last age appeared in Japan in the Nara or Early
Heian period, but it remained inside the Buddhist Order. It did not
influence general society greatly. However, in the eleventh century when
the destruction of the social order appeared, the concept of the Last Age
came to be active in actual social life.

In China, it was Hsin Hsing, originator of *Sangai* (Three-stages) doctrine, who for the first time at the end of the sixth century gave a definite form of belief to the thought of the Last Age which had been felt from the end of the Southern Dynasties. He started from the consciousness that Ages of the Right and Counterfeit *Dharma* had passed and the Last Age had begun. In this "third stage" salvation was not possible by particular Buddhas or sutras, such as *Amida* or the *Hokekyô* (Lotus sutra). He taught the veneration of actual men, as those beings who have the capacity to become Buddhas, either Buddhas of Buddha nature or future Buddhas. He taught men to worship every man or woman that they met on the road without discrimination. Though his Order had a very severe discipline, such as begging and eating only one meal a day, it was at the same time very realistic and active so that people followed him joyously. The government together with established Orders, feeling insecure, persecuted and annihilated the group about the beginning of the eighth century. The way in which the teaching *Sangai* was based on the consciousness of ignorance and wickedness which conformed to the Last Age had a great influence on the direction which later Buddhism took especially in the establishment of *Jôdo* (Pure Land) teaching.

The idea of the Pure Land had been known from old in Japan but the teaching of the Pure Land which grew within the *Tendai* sect in the Heian period has had an important significance for succeeding generations. I will leave the detailed discussion till later. Here I would mention the case of Hônen as an example of an attitude in receiving Buddhism.

Hônen ascended Hiei at the age of fifteen and studied the complicated philosophy of the *Tendai* sect from three major writings of *Tendai*. At the age of eighteen he received the baptism of *Nembutsu* under the master, Jigenbô Eikû, in Kurodani in Saito on Mount Hiei. This determined the direction of his life. It was then that he was named Hônenbô Genkû. (Judging from the fact that he used this name all through his life, we may say from the custom of the time that he didn't change his fundamental viewpoint.) It appears that his later study and practice was an effort to define whether the *Nembutsu* faith was right or wrong. He is said to have shut himself up in Kurodani for six years, perusing all the sutras several times. After he was twenty-four, he studied the doctrines of *Hosshô*, *Sanron*, *Shingon*, *Ritsu*, *Kegon*, etc., in Nara and Kyoto. It is also said that as a result of these endeavors he read the *Ôjôyôshû* by Eshin Sôzu (the Abbot of Eshin-in) and went back to the commentary of Chinese Shan T'ao. At last in 1175 at the age of forty-three he took single hearted refuge in the formula *Nembutsu*, forsaking every other practice and established the *Jôdo* sect. Hônen's standpoint is called *Senjaku* or selection. It means to "select" out the superior and "abandon" the inferior. By this method the Japanese "single-hearted practice of *Nembutsu*" was established whereby one forsakes the various ways of Buddhism and intones exclusively and verbally *Namu Amida Butsu*, that is, "Adoration to the Buddha of Infinite Life and Light."

Hônen's attitude in accepting Buddhism did not start from the motive of grasping the original and genuine form of Buddhism. Rather he intended to grasp the forms most suitable to his times. This attitude fits his character by which he gently guided those whom he met. In this sense we must call him a great religionist. Hence, the standard of his selection did not lie in truthfulness but in utility. In other words, he sought the salvation corresponding to the times and the people's capacity, giving up the pursuit of absolute truth. By this new direction, we cannot deny, the road to a new salvation was opened. At the same time, the fundamental merit of Buddhism, that is, the idea of *Bodhi*-mind was totally abandoned.

Criticism against Hônen's sole practice of *Nembutsu* came from Myôe Shônin Kôben, representative of traditional Buddhism. Kôben at first thought that it was praiseworthy, when he heard that Hônen was guiding the people with the *Nembutsu*. But after reading Hônen's *Senjakushû*, he was surprised to learn that the sole practice of *Nembutsu* was Hônen's true concept. It was in the year 1212, the year of Hônen's death, when Kôben started writing the *Zaijarin* in three volumes on hearing that the followers of *Senjû-nembutsu* would come to him for discussion. In this book, he pointed out that the *Senjû-nembutsu* was a misinterpretation from the standpoint of Buddhism. Especially, he related that the following two points held by Hônen were difficult to admit. One is the negation of the *Bodhi*-mind. The other is the theory that the *Shôdômon* (literally Holy Path teaching, or all Buddhist teachings other than Pure Land) is like a thief who hampers the right Pure Land faith.

After Hônen's death, the Pure Land teaching prevailed in the country with great force. Nichiren attacked it from an entirely different viewpoint. He said, "During the reign of Gotoba-in a man called Hônen wrote the *Senjakushû*. That is, he damaged the sacred teachings expounded in Buddha's lifetime, and misled sentient beings of the ten quarters universally (*Risshô-Ankokuron*)." Nichiren's greatest foes in his life were the followers of the *Nembutsu*.

Nichiren's thought also was based on the concept of the Last Age like the followers of Pure Land teaching, but his primary interest was not so much in individual salvation, as the national and political crisis. Taking up the cases of natural disasters, earthquakes, famine, disease and invasion of external enemies, he attributed their causes to the prevalence of Pure Land teaching. According to Nichiren, the right religion in Japan was the faith in the *Hokekyô* and owing to the encouragement of *Nembutsu,* disregarding the *Hokekyô* "the guardian good gods have gone away. This was caused solely by Hônen's *Senjakushû*." That is, the *Hokekyô* was the most genuine scripture, and therefore the national gods were angry with the abandonment of Śākyamuni, who was the preacher of that sutra and the encouragement of faith in *Amida* Buddha. Hence, there followed national disasters.

Nichiren's insistence arose by relating the faith in the *Hokekyô* to the shamanistic gods peculiar to Japan. He aimed at nationalistic political activity. Therefore, while his teaching diverged from the original stream of Buddhism, Nichiren himself believed it was the right way of Buddhism. Nichiren was bred in a fishing village along the eastern seaboard where shamanism was popular, and he grew surrounded by various spirits of popular belief. In his student days he mainly learned *Tendai* doctrine. He says, "During fifteen years, I studied all the holy scriptures of the Buddha's life and perused both Buddhist and non-Buddhist scriptures."

The ideas of the Last Age and "Selection" are common to Hônen and

Nichiren. The former thought about individual salvation and became introspective, whereas the latter was nationalistic, insisting on the accord of politics and religion and shamanistically attributed various disasters to the wrath of the gods. However, both the *Nembutsu* (*Amida*-pietism) and the *Daimoku* (*Hokke* faith) had great weight in later Japanese Buddhism and played an important role in determining its direction.

With the People

We must not forget the fact that among those who appeared to stand against the tradition of genuine Buddhism, there were many who plunged themselves among the people and enriched their lives, both materially and spiritually. Many of them were the preachers of the Pure Land faith. They, however, didn't propagate any specific sect or abuse other sects, as distinct from the founders of great sects which continued in succeeding generations. Such people gave themselves up and prayed only for the welfare, physically and mentally, of the people. Therefore, they didn't need any systematic doctrine or arguments. The reason they encouraged *Nembutsu* was simply that it was an easy practice for the people. In this way, as far as they considered it to be to the benefit of the people, they never hesitated to adopt even vulgar faith. Thus far they are closer to the method of guidance of followers in original Buddhism. It is rather ridiculous in Buddhism to discuss *Jiriki* (salvation by one's merit work) and *Tariki* (salvation by faith coming from another being). In this sense, we will offer a few who fall in the fourth category.

First, there was Kûya, "Saint of the Market" in the tenth century. His lineage is doubtful but he became a priest in his youth, walked around the country, constructed roads and bridges, repaired old temples, dug wells and buried dead bodies lying in the wilderness. Doing such things, he worked for the people and spent his life of seventy years teaching the *Nembutsu*. He had profound scholarship, but his character had great influence on the people even in later generations.

At about the same time as Kûya there seem to have been many who devoted themselves to the benefit of people, irrespective of sect. A story

is told, for example, of Genbin Sôzu of the *Hossô* sect and Riman, a follower of the *Hokekyô*. Both of them served as pilots of ferry boats. It
reminds us of the story of *Siddhartha* by Herman Hesse or Flaubert's
St. Julian.

There are some popular religionists who have been called, *hijiri* (sages)
or *shônin* (saints) in the Kamakura period. Among them, Ippen Shônin
Chishin is the most outstanding. He studied in the *Seizan* school of
Jôdoshû besides coming into contact with the doctrines of *Tendai* and
Zen and Shintoist faith. He edified people in the country with practices,
not with doctrine. He danced while reciting *Nembutsu* with the people.
Hence it is called the "Dancing *Nembutsu*" (*Odori Nembutsu*). There is
a deep meaning in the fact that Ippen who studied difficult profound
doctrine danced with the people. (The origin of the *Bon odori*, popular
in later generations, is attributed to him.) His religious group was later
described as *Jishû* (時宗), but in earlier days it was called *Jishû* (時衆).
These terms probably meant that his was not an ordinary sect. His successors also made a point of walking around and were called *Yugyô
Shônin* or wandering saints. Later, the headquarters was placed in
Shôjôkôji temple or *Yugyôji* in Fujisawa, but the influence in the country
of this sect does not attain that of former days. The truth seems to be that
the achievements of these wandering saints who contributed most con-
spicuously to the popularization of *Nembutsu* throughout the country
were also eroded by more highly organized sects with secular power.
In this way, Japanese Buddhism in modern times has become more and
more formalized, showing a tendency, so to speak, of concentrating in
monopolistic systems.

Four Types of Representative Buddhists

In the above I have distinguished four categories in respect to the attitude of those who adopted Buddhism in Japan.

In the first category, were those who sought the truth with the intention of pursuing throughly the genuine features of Buddhism. They
achieved outstanding results, both in theory and practice, by overcom-

ing many obstacles in linguistic study and in discipline. The genuineness
of their inquiries is worthy of notice in the light of up-to-date knowledge
gained in comparative studies. In their attitudes and way of life with
respect to the people as well, they realized the spirit handed down from
Śākyamuni.

The second type were those who likewise practiced the ideal of self-
lessness to the extreme, living in the tradition of Śākyamuni's Order of
monks. They appeared to be negativistic, but in reality, they stood on a
firm basis, both theoretically and practically. They brightened the people's mind with a noble attitude toward life, and also aided them in their
living.

In the third category were those who selected out something special
that they thought would be most suitable for the time from among
numerous tendencies in Buddhism. They stood on the consciousness of
crisis, and put prime importance on the sense of security for their own
minds.

In the fourth category were those who sought only the happiness of
the people, considering historical and dogmatic knowledge to be of
secondary importance. Therefore, they were more helpful for the people
in the matter of practice than in matters of theory. Their attitude to life
can be said to be common to the original spirit of Buddhism.

Those priests, who fall in the four categories, were all creative persons
who continued sincere efforts based on their own faith, throughout their
lives. Those names which I have mentioned above are but a few examples. In fact there are many priests in each category.

Besides them, there are numerous priests who don't belong to any of
these categories. They were living within the frame of a sect that was
made by other persons. They were, as it were, the people who live with
inertia. They were not frequently enthusiastic about their calling and
never tried to cultivate a new spiritual environment. They simply rested
on the laurels of previous generations. A similar phenomenon appears
not only in Buddhism, but in other religions also. When the people who
are creative, active, and always act positively, are far less in number than
those who are not, the group as a whole becomes inactive. This can be

said of Buddhism as a whole, and also of specific groups in it. One of the reasons for the recent inactivity of Buddhism may lie in this point. I am not discussing the merits of the four types. In any case, if there are many who continue in sincere efforts, a way to the solution can naturally be found. I will repeat, the foundation of Buddhism is not so much doctrine as the practice aimed at the perfection of one's self and others.

CHAPTER II

The Actual State of Japanese Buddhism

Buddhism which was established at the end of the sixth century B.C. went through frequent changes even within India. Sometime about the beginning of the Christian Era, it reached Central Asia, and finally in the first century A.D. it reached China by traveling along the trade route called "the Silk Road." From China it came to Japan through the Korean peninsula. Later, however, it was transmitted directly from China to Japan. On its way it had already undergone regional and ethnic changes passing through a number of stages. When it came to Japan, it further acquired the special coloring of the Japanese people.

That Buddhism spread in India and in the regions adjoining India was due to the contact between groups of people. Materials relating to the actual state of affairs of the Buddhist Order before King Asoka of the Mauryan dynasty in the third century B.C. are lacking, but it is certain that people before King Asoka entered into this faith. Moreover, since King Kanishka of the Kushana dynasty, which ruled Northwest India around the second century, A.D., was a foreign ruler, he had to accept the Buddhism which the native peoples believed. It appears that in the time of the kings of the later Gupta dynasty and also King Harsha, it was the people who were zealous concerning Buddhism rather than the kings.

However, when Buddhism came to China and was separated by a great distance from its fatherland, the conditions became completely altered. It was the rulers and their families who first came in contact with the officials of foreign countries, merchants, or Buddhist priests. It is

said in the *Book of the Later Han* (*Hou han shu*) that Chu Wang Ying
in P'eng Ch'eng, east of Loyang believed in Buddhism, and he was the
younger brother by a different mother of the later Han Emperor Ming
ti. About the middle of the second century in the time of Huan ti performance of rites for worshipping Huang ti, Lao tzu and Buddha and
festivals dedicated to the *Chin jen* (Golden Man, a bronze Buddha image)
spread among the royalty and nobility in the court.

Coming to the middle of the sixth century, it was a similar situation
also when Buddhism was transmitted to Japan. The Buddhist images
and texts, which were given first as gifts from the King of Kudara to
the Emperor of Japan, were primarily useful to the Emperor and the
nobles. It was the exclusive privilege of the ruling class to adorn glittering
Buddhist images and to permit the performance of foreign religious rites
rich in emotion. The rulers built temples and monasteries and trained
priests for the sake of their own happiness, or in order to hold masses for
the respose of the spirits of their ancestors. This was the beginning of
Japanese Buddhism.

Later, this curious, foreign religion was transmitted gradually from
the middle class of society to the lower classes also. There were doubtless
also occasions when it was learned directly by contact with foreign im-
migrants. It is necessary to call particular attention to two facts in order
to understand the special character of Japanese Buddhism. They are:
(1) Japanese Buddhism in its origin was not from the lower classes, but
began from the highest class of society. (2) Also those people did not
enter the Order voluntarily, but monks were made in order to perform religious rites for the ruling class. There are no examples of either
aspect in India or elsewhere. Considering these two points alone it is
clear that the mode of acceptance of Buddhism in Japan was already
from the beginning wide of the mark.

This was unavoidable with respect to Japan which was separated from
foreign nations by the sea and, therefore, was not blessed with opportu-
nities to contact foreign peoples directly. It is well to consider together
with this that after Meiji, Christianity and even the proletarian move-

ment were frequently begun by the hand of people belonging to upper class families.

However, in foreign countries there are many examples in which the reception of religion, not only Buddhism, generally began with the people and extended upward. Even in the case of the inroads of Christianity in Rome, this religion was the ally of the poor and weak and in about three hundred years it conquered Rome and brought about the conversion of Emperor Constantine.

Since Japanese Buddhism, from the beginning, developed in connection with the ruling class, even at the present time it has not freed itself completely from this characteristic which has passed through many changes. The passive attitude, which indicates that it preserves a close relationship with rulers, people of influence and wealthy persons, and stands under their patronage, is strong. It is only on very rare occasions that it is able to separate itself from these relationships and acquire freedom, both economically and spiritually.

As the religion of the rulers, of first importance was magic which aimed at increasing the happiness of the individual ruler or his family line and to avoid misfortunes. From the fact that the ruler and the nation which he ruled were viewed as one, prayers concerning the good or ill of the nation became important. It is because of this fact that Japanese Buddhism was frequently associated with nationalism.

When a religion is newly imported from a foreign country, it is common that it gives rise to friction with the long-established religions of the land, but when Buddhism arrived in Japan, the appearance of discord was seldom seen. The opposition of the Mononobe clan was subdued (587 B.C.) and the status of Buddhism came to be guaranteed through the establishment of the political power of the Soga clan. Even in the case of the opposition of the Mononobe clan, it was not a refutation with respect to the new religious thought, but it was only a struggle over the superiority or inferiority of the foreign gods and the Japanese gods. It is said that even for the Soga clan there was no interest in, or understanding of, the Buddhist doctrine, but they only adopted Buddhism from complete self-interest in which the view was expressed that there appeared to be greater efficacy in worshipping in addition (to the native gods) the exotic foreign gods. Even the Emperor of that time, from entirely the same standpoint, either adopted both Buddhism and Shintoism together or rejected one of them.

Chiefly this self-calculation determined the attitude of accepting or rejecting Buddhism. It was decided with the spread of epidemics and extermination of them, or natural calamities and upheavals as the standard of judgment. Here lies the second special characteristic of Japanese Buddhism. The ancient Japanese, similar to many ancient societies and primitive peoples, regarded the happiness or misery of individuals or society as the results of actions of unseen beings. There were infinite invisible spirits in the mountains, rivers and forests of the world of nature, and they believed that the spirits of ancestors, and dead spirits, generally, participated in the good or ills of mankind. They called these spirits *Kami*. Religious rituals were regarded as essential in order to seek the blessings of the *Kami* or, more frequently, to avoid the curse of the *Kami*. It was recognized that the newly imported Buddhism was efficacious and excelled the earlier primitive Shintoism. In this sense, Buddhist magic further performed an important service through every period until the present time. Shinto, even today, still performs magical rites. It solemnizes the New Year, prays for an abundant harvest, for the safety of new homes and construction (even on the ship Sôya which was recently headed on a scientific investigation at the South Pole a god-shelf was provided), and in general, it is employed to prevent disasters. It was believed, however, that Buddhism was more effective for such things as disasters which had already occurred, treatment of diseases and praying for rain. Through the importation of Buddhism, the types and application of Japanese magic were strikingly amplified.

We may offer rituals on behalf of the dead as the third characteristic of Japanese Buddhism. Since the Japanese lived as settled agriculturalists from ancient times, the connection of the individual and the family line was absolute, and individual consciousness was weak. Consequently, the ancestor worship of the family unit had an important meaning, and ceremonies for the dead were highly valued. This is clear from the record of the regulations governing tombs and burials, but the Japanese had only a vague idea concerning the world of the hereafter. Buddhism which was transmitted from China brought a complicated knowledge concerning man's destiny after death and taught forms of elegant ceremonials for the dead. Of course, in the beginning they were luxuries permitted only to the upper classes. But gradually Buddhist rituals reached the lower classes of society. Also, through the efforts of monks who traveled through the provinces, they were popularized. On top of that, because they were stimulated by the emergence of new sects, since the Kamakura period, Buddhist funeral ceremonies have become universal. Through the policies of the Edo Shôgunate, the family registers of the dead were entrusted to Buddhist temples. Henceforth, Buddhism and ceremonies for the dead turned out to have an inseparable relationship.

We must give the compromising spirit as the fourth character of Japanese Buddhism. As we related before, Buddhism was tolerant from the beginning of its establishment. Because of that, even in India, it was reconciled to Hinduism and eventually lost its existence as Buddhism. In China this tendency was also excessive. At the present time most Chinese frequently believe Buddhism and Taoism simultaneously, but on this point the Japanese are even more carefree. The Japanese consider the gods and Buddhas on the same level and in both modern and ancient times they participated alike in the rites of Shintoism and Buddhism. At the time of the Meiji Restoration, Shintoism and Buddhism were divided, but the attempt to make Shintoism the national religion ended in failure. Since these two religions developed interrelatedly and mutually supplemented each other, it could not be expected that they could be distinguished in the actual life of the people.

That Shintoism took a form which constituted it as a single religion was a later development, but from early times Taoism and Confucianism were in the position of competing with Buddhism. It gave rise to the problem whether these three religions imported from the continent could cooperate. The greater part of the Buddhists held the view that the three religions could ultimately be unified. Only in the case of a few opinions was the uniqueness of Buddhism in relation to the other two teachings emphasized. Among Buddhists, consequently, there were few persons who investigated the other religions. In modern times, even though Christianity has entered the scene, it has been rare that attacks have begun from the side of Buddhism.

There were also strong points in such a compromising attitude, but generally, it was easy to promote a tendency where zeal and earnestness of faith were absent.

Fifthly, one might say that Japanese Buddhism has fallen into a formalism and its true nature has been forgotten. The Indian Buddhist Order revered a simple way of life, and the monks' clothes were of one color, yellowish brown. Their possessions remained at the lowest level of life requirements. Since they did not perform rituals in order to be observed by others, they were not concerned with putting on an appearance. Even in the case of observing the percepts, they were for their own elevation and not for the sake of ostentation. In the Buddhism that came to Japan from China, monks even wore gold brocaded stoles over multi-colored robes. It was absolutely prohibited for the Indian monks to possess money. In Japan it was frequently the case that the observance of precepts was a matter of appearance. The temples and monasteries just became places of entertainment for sightseers rather than places of discipline for the monks. Since such a tendency was present from the beginning of the transmission of Buddhism to Japan, even though a few persons were correct in their discipline, in most cases they did not continue in this permanently.

With such an attitude it is natural that religious activity was completely degraded simply to recreation having no spiritual meaning. All of the activities such as going to the temple in Spring and Fall, visiting cemeteries, pilgrimages to the main temple of a sect with a religious association, were diversions which served also as picnics. We cannot say that they are not religious activities, but it is probably one of the special features of the Japanese that they do not distinguish religion and amusement.

To summarize what we have related above, the characteristics of Japanese Buddhism are: (1) Nationalism, (2) Magical Nature, (3) Ceremonies for the Dead, (4) Compromising Spirit, (5) Formalism. What did representative Buddhists think of these points? What did they do? We will consider this next.

Buddhism and Nationalism

India, in the time of the establishment of the Buddhist Order, was divided into regional governments, and since a unified nation had not appeared as yet, a national consciousness was generally lacking. The monks of the primitive Order could devote themselves entirely to the religious life and transcend the secular world. After the setting up of the Mauryan dynasty, great empires made their appearance. When it came about that the Buddhist Order received the protection of the Emperor, there appeared within Buddhism the concept that Buddhism protects the nation (*Gokoku shisô*). Sutras were produced which appear to praise monarchical government. In Central Asia and China such a tendency in Buddhism was welcomed from the start, and it was the same also in Japan.

In the golden age of the Nara court in Japan Tôdaiji temple was built. The great Buddha was constructed. And in the provinces provincial temples (*kokubunji*) were established. By these means the power of the government was backed by the authority of Buddhism. The *Kegonkyô* (*Avatansaka Sūtra*) which was the ideology behind the Tôdaiji was a text which represented, aesthetically, a systematic, unified universal order. It also became at the same time the symbol of a unified nation.

When Nara Buddhism, which had been protected and nurtured by the state, grew too rapidly, the government was forced to move the capital to Heiankyô (Kyoto). In the new capital also a new Buddhism was required. It was the *Tendai* school of Saichô and the *Shingon* school of Kûkai which answered this demand. As Saichô frequently said, "To cause the *Dharma* to abide eternally is to protect the nation." He regarded the flourishing of Buddhism as having the tranquility of the nation as its object. Kûkai also advocated the principle that Buddhism pacifies and preserves the nation. Saichô placed *Tendai* teaching on his shingle, but he did not have as his primary objective pure *Tendai* philosophy, but rather the organization of Buddhism which would be useful to the state. Therefore he introduced together with it elements of esoteric Buddhism (*Mikkyô*). Kûkai transmitted and organized the orthodox line of *Mikkyô*. This was an elegant teaching brought from India by Amoghavajra in the time of Emperor Hsüan tsung of the T'ang dynasty. Saichô's successors also equally imported *Mikkyô* after studying abroad in T'ang China. The two schools of *Tendai* and *Shingon* competed in the Heian court, and they had great influence on the lives of the Imperial house and the nobility through performance of esoteric, magical rites. At that time *Mikkyô* acquired a status which we may call the state religion. The priests of *Mikkyô* were kept busy with such great concerns as the peace of the nation down to prayers for the cure of disease and childbirth. However, after the power of the Emperor passed into the hands of the warriors, both the centers of Mount Hiei and Mount Kôya became unable to preserve their ancient prestige. *Tendai* and *Shingon* actually were not related to the state power, but it was the case that they only relied on individual relations with Emperors and nobles. However, these two schools even to the present time cling to the standpoint that Buddhism pacifies and preserves the nation (*Chingo-kokka*). Of course, their content has changed with the times. In the medieval period, modern times and even in the Second World War, prayers for the submission of the enemy nation were the primary work of the temples belonging to these sects.

The relationship of the *Shingon* school and the Imperial House continues, though slightly, even to the present time. Every year ceremonies praying for the tranquility of the Imperial Person and the peace of the nation are performed by the hand of the *Shingon* priests. This is called *Mishiho*. In the fourth year of Meiji (1872) these rites were completely abolished, but similarly in the fifteenth year (1883) they were revived. After borrowing the Emperor's robes and offering prayers in the ceremony, the robes are returned.

It was not only the ancient Buddhists of the Nara and Heian courts who sought to approach the highest political forces of their age such as the Imperial house or the Shôgunate. The newly originated sects which began in the Kamakura period, whenever there was opportunity, tried to approach persons with political power. It is obvious in the *Rinzai Zen* school which from the beginning received protection from the Shôgunate and the Imperial court, but in addition *Jôdoshû, Jôdoshinshû* and *Nichirenshû* schools, at least those which continue today as the great sects, all, without exception, contrived at every opportunity to approach the Shôgunate and Court. The Honganji, which descends from Shinran, as a primary power of the feudal system, gradually increased its authority and from the Tembun period (after 1530) it had associations with many great Daimyô, and through the Kujô family approached the court. After Meiji it had an in-law relation with the Imperial family and, ranking with the nobles, its aristocratic status was publicly recognized.

That the *Jôdoshû* especially developed was due to the protection of the Tokugawa family. Zonnô Genyo, who is called the restorer of Zôjôji temple in Edo (Tokyo), was honored and respected by Ieyasu, and he maintained the status of Zôjôji. However, it was stated by Tsuji Zennosuke: "We cannot say that his character was noble. His actions were frequently mean." The people of that time also are noted as saying: "O how terrible, the holy priest of Zôjôji who is strong in secular affairs is not far from hell." However, not limiting to Zônnô alone, at that time there were not a few individuals who were not of the highest character among the priests who cleverly got in favor with politicians.

Nichiren's nationalism was completely distinctive of his teaching. His standpoint was that in the world of the Last Age of the *Dharma* the *Hokekyô* (Lotus Sutra) alone was the only true teaching of the Buddha (*Buppô*). Particularly he said: "The land of Japan is solely the land of the *Hokekyô*;" "All the people of Japan, for more than four hundred years since Emperor Kammu, are singularly (*ikkô*) the beings of the *Hokekyô*." Then, "Now Nichiren has done nothing else for twenty-eight years but only to strive that all the people of Japan should recite the five or seven letters *Myôhôrengekyô* alone. This is thus the compassion of a mother striving to put milk in the mouth of an infant." However, "while Chinese and Koreans have abandoned the good protective deities and become followers of *Zen* teaching and the *Nembutsu*, they have submitted to the Mongols." It is because *Zen* and *Nembutsu* teachings have flourished in China and Korea that they have been conquered by the Mongols. Even in Japan, "they have gotten rid of the good protective deities, and they seriously live according to Hônen's concept of selection (*Senjaku*). How sad it is! For fifty or sixty years millions of people have been captivated by a devilish condition (*Māra*-condition), which made them err into false beliefs in Buddhism. Will they not incur the wrath of the good deities when they have frequently gone astray in other inferior teachings, forgetting the true doctrine? Won't they obtain the support of evil spirits by rejecting the perfect and desiring the partial?" Because Hônen's *Nembutsu* teaching flourished, "calamities, natural disasters, famines and plagues fill the country and are rampant all through the land." Not only that, but "now, Japan suffers from the attempts of the Mongols to plunder it." All is as prophesied in the *Hokekyô*. However, "this fact only Nichiren alone in Japan knew." "Nichiren is the number one devotee of the *Hokekyô* in Japan." In spite of that the Shôgunate did not accept his words, but "on the contrary, they caused Nichiren to meet with various difficulties and finally banished him to this island, Sado." "Nichiren is the pillar of Japan. If they are deprived of Nichiren, they have overthrown the pillar of Japan."

We have quoted entirely Nichiren's own words above, but, while at the same time that in his expression there is excessive self-consciousness, when we look at the content, he is asserting that only he alone can save Japan through the *Hokekyô*. He also states: "This land is a divine land" and he prayed for "the peace of the land, the tranquility of the state." But because no one listened to him, "all the people of Japan, high and low entirely are the formidable enemies of the *Hokekyô*. Since it has been so for many years, great disasters pile up, and because great destructive deities have entered into every person, they are beside themselves, bereft of their right minds at the (diplomatic) notes of the Mongols."

No matter how much Nichiren strained himself, his voice only reached the ears of the lower rank of officials of the Shôgunate, and his own national concept was merely abstract, lacking in a sense of reality.

If, as he said, the nation recognized the faith of the *Hokekyô* as the only true one, and prohibited all other sects, Japan would prosper. But if not, there was nothing else except the destruction of the land. To put it in other words, it means to recognize his sect as the single state religion and to suppress all others. It is a self righteousness unexampled in all of Buddhist history, and viewed from the standpoint of Buddhist tolerance, we must say that it is a completely non-Buddhistic attitude. In spite of the fact that Nichiren made a vow from his youth to Bodhisattva (*Kokûzô*, Skt. *Akāśagarbha*) that he would become the number one teacher of Japan (it was the same with Kûkai), his intolerance was because he lacked a fundamental knowledge of Buddhism.

Nichiren died in obscurity without achieving his aspiration, but such self righteousness even in later times frequently gave rise to public criticism among other sects. The nationalism asserted by Nichiren was revived after Meiji. In the thirteenth year of Meiji (1881) the *Rengekai* (Lotus Society) of Tanaka Chigaku; later *Risshô-Ankokukai* (Society of the National Pillar) was outstanding. This society influenced politicians and military men and inspired fascism. There are many newly arisen quasi-religious fellowships deriving from the line of *Nichiren* teaching which make their platform merely individual salvation. The *Sôka Gakkai*, which is a fellowship having the outline of *Nichiren Shôshû* teaching, has determined this sect as the only state religion and has as its object the suppression of all other religions. Hence we may say that it is merely a modern edition of Nichiren nationalism. However, since Nichiren lived in obscurity all his life, he remained with only a subjective concept, and his activity never took concrete form. Because the way of thinking of Nichiren or people who draw from the stream of Nichiren is such that it associates their sect with political power and contrives to control thought and speech, we should pay attention to this point.

Among all of the representative Buddhists of Japan, Shinran indicates no direct interest in nationalistic thought. For Shinran it was probably the case, actually, that there was no opportunity to approach the court or Shôgunate. In contrast to this, it was Dôgen who, though having such an opportunity, made it his clearly announced intention to avoid approaching political authorities.

Dôgen was the son of the Home Minister (*Naidaijin*) Kuga Michichika who was related by blood to the Murakami Genji. His mother was said to be the daughter of the Regent Fujiwara Motofusa. Since he was of the nobility by birth, it was expected that even after he became a monk he could have had a relation with the nobility. However, he disdained to associate with the political authorities of Kyoto and Kamakura. It was original Buddhist principle to strive solely in pure discipline leaving out of account the political power of the nation, and this was also the true tradition which Dôgen had inherited.

He related also of his own teacher Ju ching: "He was not familiar with the Emperor, nor did he have an audience. He was not intimate with the ministers nor with the officials. . . . He not only refused the purple robe and title, but he did not wear a patterned (vari-colored) stole during his lifetime. It was common then that when ascending to the hall and entering the room, everyone used a black surplice and stole." And Dôgen himself throughout his life observed the rules of a monk. Moreover, at the time, it was considered an honor by most Buddhists to be an advisor to the Emperor, but Dôgen has this to say about it: "When an advisor of the Emperor is chosen, by no means does it signify that a righteous person has been chosen. It is hard for the Emperor to know a righteous person. He only promotes someone on hearing the recommendation of the ministers. There have been teachers of Emperors who were virtuous in the past and present, and there have been many teachers who were not righteous. Those who are promoted in the sullied generation are unvirtuous men, and those who are not promoted in the sullied age are virtuous men."

In these words there is contained a bitter criticism concerning the Buddhists of Sung China and Japan at that time, and they are words which are suitable, of course, for the present time also.

In the eighth month of 1247 Dôgen went to Kamakura after being invited, and in the next year, the third month, he returned to Eiheiji temple in Echizen. At this time Tokiyori requested Dôgen to remain in Kamakura, and he promised to establish a temple for him. However, Dôgen refused it. That temple is said to be the later Kenchôji. After that, Tokiyori offered to donate the Rokujô fort in Echizen as a fief of Eiheiji.

Dôgen not only rejected it, but he also expelled Gemmyô who was the messenger bearing the notice of this donation. It is said that (Dôgen) "cut up the floor of the (monastery) where Gemmyô performed *Zazen*, dug the earth under the floor seven foot deep in the ground and threw it away."

In the year 1250 the retired Emperor Go-Saga sent an Imperial messenger and bestowed (on Dôgen) a purple robe. Dôgen twice refused it, but on the third time he took it with reluctance. In a poem from that time he wrote:

> Even though the valley of Eiheiji is shallow,
> The Imperial command is weighty, weighty, weighty.
> All the more the monkey and crane will be made to laugh,
> If an old man (wears) the purple robe.

Hence, he put the purple robe away as it was, and never kept it about him during his whole life. Thus Dôgen cut off any connection with worldly fame and wealth and for his lifetime continued in his efforts in the original path of a monk. For Dôgen it was completely the way of the monk, and the way of a layman was different. Here he differed from most sages of the Pure Land teaching in having a clear view of government.

> According to the rules of government, everyone, all those who are in the government, from the highest prince down to the lowest common man, master their work. If they are not qualified men, their abiding in the government brings confusion to the state. When the administration accords with the will of Heaven, the people living in the world are at peace. Therefore, the Emperor rises at one a.m. and spends his time with affairs of state. He does not take his ease. From him downward to the nobles, high stewards, and common people, all have their work which they are to conduct. We say that he who follows that duty is a man. (*Shôbôgenzô-zuimonki* No. 2.)

It is a righteous government, when beginning with the Emperor, the officials and also the common people put all their efforts into their respective duties. If they turn against this, they receive the punishment of Heaven. It is the case that when the monk also strives in his discipline, he performs his duty. This was Dôgen's concept of the nation and government. There was one difference between worldly government and Buddhist discipline, according to Dôgen.

> Even though worldly rulers consider and seek the righteousness of the ancient laws, as there are no examples which have for certain been transmitted by the ancient sages and pioneers, they follow the examples of their own time. But for the Buddhist the ancient rules and teachings are clear. The knowledge of the tradition mutually received exists up to now. (From previously quoted text.)

Government decides the standard of good and evil based on precedent, and since there is no absolute law, it is flexible. However, Buddhism has a clear foundation, and since it extends till today through the tradition handed down from the masters, it has a trustworthy standard. To put it in other words, government follows empirical law, but Buddhism manifests an absolute law transcending experience. On this point, the superiority of Buddhism in contrast to the secular, to put it in a European mode of speaking, is the recognition of the superiority of philosophy in relation to government. The thought which clearly distinguishes between Buddhism and politics in Dôgen is none other than to indicate the ultimate superiority of Buddhism.

However, Dôgen's nobility was not at all faithfully inherited by his successors. His disciple of the fourth generation, Keizan Jôkin, laid the foundation of Sôjiji (at that time in Noto province, moved to Yokohama in 1899) and was highly respected by Emperor Go-Daigo. Keizan was rich in real capacity for such things as administering a temple, but with his disciple Gazan Shôseki the relationship with the court became deeper and Sôjiji developed more and more.

After that also, there were many who were revered by the Emperor, Shôguns, and Daimyô, and received the purple robe and the honorary title of Zenji. However in the *Sôtô* school lineage with Dôgen as its founder, it has been rare to see any who participated in the administration of the country.

When viewed in this way, we may say that, setting aside those Buddhists for whom there was no opportunity to approach political authorities, there have been few besides Dôgen who have preserved the noble attitude stemming from his assertion of principle. Among them, furthermore, there were also persons who participated in the administration of the government and planned the control of religion through national political power. Generally, when a new government is established, ambitious people come together. We can note the uncommon shrewdness of Zonnô on whom Ieyasu relied. But in the beginning of the Edo Shôgunate, two or three Buddhist priests made the most of the new government and distorted Buddhism considerably. They appeared to be protecting Buddhism, but actually they established a policy of interference and control. Finally Buddhism was completely emasculated.

Thus on the basis of national control, the sectarian organization and the parish system were solidified. It was (the priest) Sûden of the *Rinzai* school who caused this Buddhist policy to be formulated and executed. This person was the originator of the present Buddhist system, that is, he is remembered as the individual having the highest responsibility for the degeneration of the Buddhist temples and monasteries. Tenkai of the *Tendai* school, who was his competitor and the religious advisor through the three generations of Ieyasu, Hidetada and Iemitsu, primarily endeavored to expand the power of the *Tendai* sect and constructed the Tôshôgû shrine (the Mausoleum of Ieyasu) in Nikkô. We cannot say that it was just accidental that the Buddhist history of the Edo period, in which the curtain was raised by such political priests, was defiled by the activities of evil priests.

The new government of Meiji established Shintoism, so to speak, as the state religion and abolished the protection of Buddhism. However, the relationship of the temple and parishioners of the Edo period has remained until today, in the generally accepted social sense, as it was. As a matter of fact, its relationship with the Imperial family and nobility has continued to exist. It is a fact that Buddhism, although not equalling

Shinto, compared to Christianity and the newly arisen religious sects, was treated favorably by the authorities. The Religious Bodies Law (*Shûkyô Dantai Hô*) enacted in 1939 was convenient for the already existing religious communities. After the defeat of the Second World War, the Occupation Headquarters quickly caused this law to be abolished, and by Imperial Ordinance they caused the *Shûkyô Hôjin Rei* (Religious Corporation Ordinance) to be publicly promulgated. However, coming down to 1951, the Religious Juridical Persons Law (*Shûkyô Hôjin Hô*) was enacted. The outstanding feature of this law is that it completely frees religion from the control of the state (to speak more concretely, the *Mombushô*, Education Ministry). Instead of the prewar license system, it adopted the report system. This was based on the principle of freedom of belief which was guaranteed by the new Constitution, and it was convenient for Christianity and the new religions. However, it was disadvantageous for Shintoism which had come to be protected previously by the state and political authorities secretly and openly. There was also no rejoicing at this from the side of the Buddhist temples as already established groups. We can observe a movement which would turn for the worse in the direction of religious control by the state paralleling a recent retrogressive trend. So far as it concerns Buddhism, the framework of control enacted in the beginning of Edo was, doubtless, at least desirable for the powerful temples.

Magic and Prayer

No matter what the religion, there are, to begin with, few which do not contain elements of magic. It cannot be said that there are absolutely no vestiges of magic except in special cases even in Protestantism which might have been expected to liquidate the magical elements so numerous in medieval Catholicism. Further, the role which magic plays in the religion of a society which does not have such self-reflection is very great. Also, it cannot be denied that both in primitive and modern societies magic has a religious appeal for most people.

In Japanese religious existence Buddhist elements were added to ancient primitive Shinto, Shrine Shinto and *Onyôdô* (a tradition of divination introduced from China in the seventh century), and a complicated combination of magic developed to the present day. The government tried to divide Buddhism and Shintoism in 1868, but in actual life these elements could not be strictly distinguished. Actually, there is an attitude in men which demands magic. There is no objection to its being Buddhism, Shintoism or some other form of religion, if it will fulfil this demand.

When Buddhism was first transmitted in the middle of the sixth century, the Japanese did not take notice of what kind of doctrine or ethics it possessed. They only paid attention to the question of how useful the Buddha image, which was a new foreign god, would be in preventing calamity or increasing happiness. Through the conditions of the spread of plagues, they either worshipped the Buddha image or rejected it.

Later, there did appear individuals who studied Buddhist doctrine and ethics, and Japanese spiritual life became rich. There were also not a few who grasped Buddhism theoretically and practically. Despite that, nevertheless, most believers, as even today, understood Buddhism as a magical religion. On this point, we must recognize on the one hand, that Buddhism possessed the possibility of becoming a magical religion, and, on the other hand, we must admit that it was the Japanese people, who, on their part, required such a religious form.

Buddhism had as its original object the enabling of man through his ability, to cause his *Bodhi* mind to grow and to proceed toward an ideal state. Consequently, it does not disavow the natural state of man, but rather teaches advancement having that natural state as its foundation. Therefore, Buddhism never radically destroys man's spiritual foundation, but a method is selected to convert that foundation to a higher ideal perspective. In this sense, Śākyamuni did not abolish magic for either lay believers or monks so far as it was not direct harm. Even in the Order he publicly recognized incantations for protection against snakes. The reason for this is that if one advances to a higher spiritual level, each person becomes awakened to his true self and such things will become no longer necessary.

Such a tolerant attitude on the part of Śākyamuni, at a later age, resulted in the introduction into Buddhism of many diverse elements of popular belief. This was all the more the case in Mahayana Buddhism which tries to discover the ideal state within actuality itself. Then it was *Mikkyô* which established a Pan-Buddhistic view of the world (*Hanbutsuron*, the concept that identifies the universe with Buddha) in combination with various elements. It pushed the Mahayana principle that "the Real is the Ideal" (*Genjitsu-soku-Risô*), and it extensively affirmed human existence. Because *Mikkyô* states that Passion is *Bodhi* (*Bonnô-soku-Bodai*) and grasps Reality even with its weak points as the ideal state, both human instincts and the magic which fulfils those demands were accepted within perfection as a whole. These various elements were only one part of a harmonious whole.

However, such a conception of the world based upon the esoteric Buddhism, when viewed from the eyes of most people, was merely a mass of superstitions. Especially during the period when Buddhism came to China and Japan, the Buddhist character of *Mikkyô* was lost sight of, and it was frequently the case that the magic of popular belief was assimilated to it. A few men like Kûkai succeeded in grasping systematically the *Mikkyô* world view, but the greater number simply saw the magic alone as the constitutive element. Thus, from the onset of the Heian court until later times, the *Mikkyô* of the *Shingon* and *Tendai* schools had as its function the magical compliance with the demands of the general populace. *Tendai*, which was centered on Mount Hiei, attained an increasingly strong coloring of *Mikkyô* after the death of Saichô. Beginning with the priests Ennin and Enchin, all those who studied in T'ang China transmitted *Mikkyô* magic and imported its implements and texts. Hence *Tendai Mikkyô* (called *Taimitsu*) and *Shingon Mikkyô* (*Tômitsu*) competed against each other. In the Fujiwara period (9th–12th centuries A.D.) it spread among the court and nobles. In the Kamakura period (1192–1333) Nichiren deplored the fact that *Tendai* had rejected the faith of the *Hokekyô* which was its proper province and degenerated to an imitation of *Shingon*. And he denounced the *Shingon* school as an enemy. He said:

Especially the *Shingon* school is a great disaster for this country. To
curse the great Mongols, one should not be commanded by the teachers
of *Shingon*. If the *Shingon* masters curse the great enterprise, this nation
will undoubtedly be destroyed quickly.

Nichiren did not deny the efficacy of magic itself, but it appears that
he spurned competitors and tried to offer his services as a magician. In
the drought of 1271 he carried on a contest of praying for rain with
Ninshô, a priest of *Ritsu* school, of the Gokurakuji temple. Looking at
this event, it appears that Nichiren was self-confident in his own magic.
Nichizô, who had interviews with Nichiren during his lifetime, and
when Nichiren died took the tonsure by his casket, constructed the
Myôkenji temple in Kyoto which was officially acknowledged as Imperial Prayer House in 1333. In 1336 he was requested by Ashikaga
Tadayoshi to pray for the Shôgun's family. Further, Daikaku, who was
the successor of Nichizô, also frequently prayed for the Shôgun being
commissioned by Tadayoshi and Yoshiakira. Consequently even though
Nichiren never occupied himself with magic, it is certain that such a
tendency already existed from the beginning. In reality, in later times,
there were not a few of *Nichiren* sect lineage who made magic their
business. Even at the present time among the new quasi-religions which
make their object the cure of disease, and business prosperity, the so-called
worldly benefits (*genzeriyaku*), very many are of *Nichiren* lineage.

This is not a condition of the *Nichiren* sect alone, but *Zen* temples also
frequently traveled the same route of destiny. In the time of Emperor
Go-Daiko (1325), beginning with the Daitokuji temple which became
a *gokiganjo* (a place of prayer and vows), many among the large and
small temples complied with the demands of the warriors as places of
prayer. The *Zen* temples which were in the beginning centers for the
practice of *Zazen*, responding to the requests of believers, became places
of prayer and later *bodaisho* (places in which one prays for the enlightenment of ancestors). Later it was the general tendency of *Zen* temples
that their character as *bodaisho* became strong. Likewise, in recent times
most of the religious sects became accommodated to this general
tendency.

It was the various sects of *Jôdo* (Pure Land) lineage and particularly *Jôdo Shinshû* (True Sect of the Pure Land) which followed Shinran, which rejected worldly benefit and abolished magic.

In the teaching of Shinran who purified further Hônen's *Senju-nembutsu* (Sole Practice of Recitation of Amida Buddha's Name), it was not permitted to believe in anything outside of *Amida Buddha*. Quoting the following passage, he taught that one should not venerate the gods and spirits of other religions or believe in lucky and unlucky days:

> The *Hanjuzammai Sutra* (Sutra on the *Samādhi* called *Pratyutpanna*) states: "When female devotees desire to study after hearing this *Samādhi.* . . . Let them take refuge in the Buddha, in the *Dharma* and in the *Sangha*. Be careful not to serve other religions, worship Heaven (here, gods of India), or to venerate the dead spirits, or to look for lucky and auspicious days."

However, it is not the case that Shinran denied the existence of the gods (*Kami*) as a popular belief, but he appears to have recognized their existence:

> All the gods who reside in heaven protect those who believe deeply in the Buddhist *Dharma* as the shadow follows the form.

In any case, among the Buddhist sects of Japan it was *Shinshû* that became free of magic. Since it came about that the priests of this sect established their livelihood through rituals for the dead, as we will relate in the next section, it was probably not necessary economically to rely on the remunerations of magic.

What threatened the men of primitive societies were the various spirits such as living spirits, dead spirits and nature spirits. Man's environment was filled with these invisible existences. Plagues, disasters, and individual misfortunes were all the work of spirits. Even in the Heian court which appears in one aspect gay and brilliant, there was not much difference from primitive societies on this point. After that, even to the present time, the spirits have controlled in a part of Japanese society. This condition probably resulted from the fact that the greater part of the Japanese maintained a close relation with the land and family and were not completely freed from the domination of ancient spirits. It also resulted from the fact that there lacked a habit of investigating scientifically the law of cause and effect. The number of persons, who unconsciously rely on the worship of fetishes and stick to auspicious days and taboos, while being disinterested in religious thought, is surprisingly great.

The *goma* service (rite of offering incense and prayer; in Sanskrit, *homa*) is a conspicuous ceremony of magic in Buddhism. Originally, it was a method of making an offering to the gods, according to the rules of Indian Brahmins, and seeking good fortune, but it was adopted by *Mikkyô* and transmitted to Japan. While the Heian court was flourishing the nobles worshipped the *Godai-Myôô* (Five Law guardians of the Five Dhyāni-Buddhas) providing five altars and caused the priests to perform prayers and austerities:

> Because the time (of delivery of the Prince) drew near, they performed numberless magical prayers. They carried out the ceremonies of the five honored ones (*Goson, Godai Myôô*). All the clothes and actions following the various rites appeared just so. The Abbot of Kannon-in and twenty priests performed incantations by various means. . . . Shinyo Ajari wore a red robe according to the *Gundari* rite. Saigi Ajari bowed in reverence to Dai-i-toku (Yamantaka). The Abbot of Ninnaji temple performed the ceremonies according to the *Kujaku* sutra. One after another they did these things until dawn (Chapter *Hatsuhana* in *Eiga Monogatari*).

Because the Heian nobles staked their destinies on the fact that their daughters would bear a son for the Emperor, they thus carried out extravagant magical rites.

Generally the *goma* rite which venerated the Lord *Fudô-myôô* (*Acalanātha*) was most frequently performed. After the Kamakura period it was not infrequent that it was imitated by sects other than *Shingon* and *Tendai*. From the Edo period it became closely associated with popular religion, and particularly the Shinshôji temple of Narita in Chiba became famous as the object of faith of the Edo townspeople.

Ganeśa, a god of fortune originating in Hinduism was accepted into Buddhism and called Lord of Joy (*Kangiten*), and generally in Japan is known as *Shôden* (*Daishô Kangiten*). In India, even today, he is broadly believed in as a god who has charge of wisdom and good fortune. He has the figure of a man with the head of a one-tusked elephant, but images of a double-bodied "Lord of Joy" in the form of a man and woman in embrace are frequent. The *Shôden* of Hôzanji on Mt. Ikoma, Nara, has become the object of worship for the merchants of Kansai.

Kishimojin also is widely known as an object of popular, magical faith. This deity was the wife of a destructive spirit and named in Sanskrit, *Hārītī*. She always took people's children and ate them. Śākyamuni hid her youngest child and instructed her that she would get her child back by promising never to kill a human child. This legend appears in various sutras. From ancient times in India she was believed in as a goddess of birth and actually in the Gandhara region beautiful sculptures have been discovered. In China she is believed in as the "Mother Goddess of Nine Children" (*Kishimojin*). There are many Chinese-style images of this goddess which have been transmitted also to Japan. In the chapter on spells of the *Hokekyô* it is stated:

> These ten female spirits came to the Buddha together with the whole family of *Kishimojin* and her children, and altogether they spoke, "O World Honored One, we also would like to protect those who read and remember the *Hokekyô* so that they do not become troubled."

On the basis of this appeal they have become the principal magical images of deities particularly protecting infants and are worshipped in temples of the *Nichiren* sect. Hokekyôji temple of Nakayama in Chiba is especially famous.

Besides that, various sacred images are enshrined everywhere. The principal object of magic can be said to consist of three types such as health and longevity, prosperity, and curses. Cursing is used even today in time of war.

Incantations are an accessory to magical practice. The belief that there is mystical power confined in words is worldwide. They are transmitted as secret formula among special Buddhist priests. In many cases the reading of sutras is expected to have a magical effect. The fact that Chinese texts are recited even today where they are meaningless to the hearers and not intelligible at all to the reading monks may be viewed on one side as something concerned with magical efficacy.

Besides the Chinese texts, incantations with Sanskrit origins are frequently used. Among them some like *Onabiraunken-sowaka* (*om-a-vi-ra-hūm-kham svāhā*) are transmitted among the people, and there are also some which are employed among other things for stopping tooth-aches. The phrases *Namu-Amida-Butsu* (*Jôdo* sect) and *Namu-Myôhô-Renge-Kyô* (*Nichiren* sect) have been used for similar purposes.

More important than those incantations are the mythical objects. These are not restricted only to Buddhism but among the Japanese it is frequent even now that people depend on amulets as a manifestation of magical power which can be touched with the hand. They are objects such as a flat piece of paper or a piece of board on which has been inscribed the name of a god or Buddha, or a word and diagram. It is believed that through them one can avoid disasters of an evil spirit and invite good fortune. There are various kinds to avoid disaster such as fire, water, insects, lightning, etc., but they change according to the demand of the times. Most recently there have frequently appeared amulets to protect against automobile accidents. Bettering one's fortune, easy delivery in birth and safety within the home are the same now as in ancient times. Sometimes they are affixed to the body, stuck to the door, or taken like medicine. There is very little difference between Buddhism and Shintoism concerning the use of amulets.

Reverence for sacred objects was present also in Indian Buddhism. However, it was chiefly only in the faith of the lay people, and the monks were not known to participate. Śākyamuni's remains, the relics (*shari, śarīra*), were divided by the lay devotees; and stupas were constructed at ten locations. Relics, which were hard gem-like crystal, were transmitted to China also. There they became objects of devotion. It is said that under one of the cornerstones of the pagoda of Hôryûji temple in Nara a relic was dedicated. Relics were rare in Japan and, consequently they did not generally become objects of devotion. In place of that, the remains and keepsakes of famous priests became venerated. It is because of that, that

Mount Kôya, where Kûkai's remains are enshrined, the Honganji, which developed from the ancestral tomb of Shinran, and Mount Minobu, where Nichiren's remains are gathered, have become places of devotion. There is something said to be Nichiren's tooth in the Daisekiji temple at Fuji, the general main temple of the *Nichiren Shôshû* sect which has become famous most recently through the activities of the *Sôka Gakkai*.

Further, in the *Nichiren Shôshû* sect a board mandala is the basis for claiming that it is the true lineage of Nichiren. Theories that the board mandala is a forgery have also appeared, but setting aside the question of its authenticity, the faith that a part of Nichiren's physical body or his handwriting possesses magical power is a problem. Indeed, since the example of the *Sôka Gakkai* has become famous, it has gone so far as to attract the attention of the world. There are many cases in all countries of the worship of relics similar to this. The authenticity of the relics is a problem of historians, but our interest is drawn mainly to magical faith in them.

In line with the worship of relics we can also regard the worship of sages as one type of magical faith. The Japanese generally have a strong tendency to hero-worship, and the belief that one acquires super-natural power through contact with great religious persons is manifested in various areas. The faith that disease is cured just by touching the hem of a saint's robe is found among modern Japanese similar to the time of Jesus Christ. In the case of the Japanese, faith is great in the high priests and princely heads of great temples and monasteries, and the thought of submission to the powerful is strong. The rite of "Shaving" which is performed in *Jôdo Shinshû* is also a case of this, and we may say that it follows the rule of contact of sympathetic magic of which the ethnologists have spoken. In the case of the prohibition of magic in such groups as *Jôdo Shinshû*, we may see that the worship of individuals has come back as a substitute for fetish worship.

As we have seen above, in almost every aspect of Japanese Buddhism magical faith is alive. Its extent and type vary. But there are things which must be considered here. Goethe has said:

There are only two kinds of true religion. One of them is the religion
in which we recognize and revere the holiness which lies in and around us
completely apart from form. Another is the religion which recognizes
and reveres (it) in the most beautiful form. That which is neither of them
is idolatry.

Magic originally arose from the psychology of uncivilized man, but
the desire to grasp the holy and the sublime through form also exists in
us. When magic is purified and elevated, mystical thought and ceremony
develops. If we cannot grasp it at all apart from form, may we not make
our existence bright and radiant through religious ritual which manifests
beautiful harmony? Actually, the beautiful Buddhist images which our
ancestors have left for us give us hope even on this point. It is probably
not unreasonable to expect of Buddhism hereafter religious rites which
will satisfy our intelligence and emotions. For that, religious ritual must
develop in a manner that harmonizes with a sound world view and view
of man, when magic based on utilitarian motives has been transcended.
I do not know whether there are such preparations in the presently
existing religious bodies.

Ceremonies for the Dead

From ancient times the Japanese have experienced various stages in
funeral rites. In the period of Jômon culture the dead person's hands and
feet were folded up and firmly tied and simply buried in a hole. This is
called *kussô* (burial by folding). The archaeologists interpret it as the
attempt to prevent the dead spirit, who is wandering about the earth,
from giving injury to people. When we come to the Yayoi period, the
dead body was placed in a casket letting it be at ease, and they covered
it on the ground with earth. A stone was placed upon it as if leaving a
landmark. This is called *shinsô* (extended burial) or *kansô* (coffin burial).
Next in the Kofun period it came about that they made *tumuli* on a grand
scale with the front square and the rear round. They were built for the
sake of the emperor and the powerful clans of the region, and among
the articles buried with them were also valuable articles. Soon the making

of tombs extended to the middle class also and became formalized. This style became obsolete. About that time Buddhism was transmitted and a new burial system began.

We can learn the way of thinking of the ancient Japanese concerning the dead person from such customs which existed before the entrance of Buddhism. First, there was the fear that the dead spirit may do injury to the living. This thought has remained in later generations also.

In order to pacify angry spirits, special religious rites were regarded as necessary. The angry spirit would bring evil not only on the party with whom he was angry in life, but also on third parties. Even if not that, since the dead person considers that his death is entirely unfortunate, it is believed that frequently he does not think pleasantly about those who remain alive.

Second was the idea of cherishing the memory of the dead person. This appears to be in contradiction with the first point, but actually it is frequent that it is carried out parallel. When a certain time has passed after death, the dead spirit, being content with his status, becomes an ancestral spirit. This appears to correspond to the time when the dead body is obliterated without trace. Thus he loses his individuality, and becomes *Kami* or "Ancestor," and after that he exerts himself for the happiness and safety of the descendants as the protecting deity of the home or birthplace. The ancestral spirit does not go away to a distant world, but he remains close by and protects the life of the descendants. He returns home at a specified time every year, and at that time the descendants gladden the ancestral spirits by offering food.

Thirdly, we may recognize as an accessory fact that the ceremonies for the dead are also carried out as a means to display the prestige of the family.

Such rites for the dead are also said to be an expression of ancestor worship, but they are not at all peculiar to Japan alone. Fustel De Coulanges has said:

> Life in the underworld does not differ greatly from the present life. Because of that the dead require food. Men offered food at a determined time in the year at the respective graves.

Modern Europeans have completely ceased the custom of providing food for the dead, but among the ancient Greeks and Romans, nevertheless, "the dead ate the food provided at the tombs and drank the wine poured out there. Consequently, it was believed that those who were not provided with anything went down to eternal starvation." (*La Cité Antique.*)

If we consider what has been written above, we can understand the spiritual basis on which the Japanese burial system which we will relate later has developed.

How was it in Indian Buddhism? Śākyamuni's community was a gathering of pure religious devotees, and they had no relation to religious rituals at all. (Refer author's *Bukkyô*, p. 126 ff. and pp. 188 ff., Iwanami Shoten, publisher.) According to Śākyamuni's clear last wish, funeral rites were entrusted to lay believers. It was because they were something which the homeless monks should not participate in. Even in India in later times there were also reading of sutras, praying to Buddha and providing flowers and incense for the sake of the dead. When a monk died, friends cremated him, and one person read the *Mujôkyô* (Sutra on Impermanence). Such practices were described by a Chinese monk, I Ching, who traveled through India around the seventh century. I Ching also recognized the fact that the funeral rites following the teaching of Śākyamuni were not as pretentious as "the secular ceremonies of Chou Kung" in Confucianism.

When we speak from the standpoint of Śākyamuni's theory, a man's destiny after death is determined by each person's actions during his life. Therefore, another person cannot participate in it. Soon a tendency to relax this extremely severe moral law appeared in some Orders. Buddha's infinite compassion had to extend to all beings. Also because the Bodhisattvas, who continue their strivings with Buddha as the idea, give absolutely everything which they possess to beings, they transfer to them even the reward of all their good deeds in the past. From such a fact the thought termed *Ekô* originated. This word means "to direct," "to turn over" (*parināma*), and is used in the sense that one confers on another person one's own merit from good deeds.

Moreover, the thought indicating the virtue of reading sutras gradually began to appear. In the ancient Buddhist Order, the sutras were studied for the sake of one's own learning, but at a later time recitation and lecturing on the Mahayana sutras were recommended as good deeds. From such a situation it came about that they called the practice of reading the sutras for the sake of other people, especially for the dead, *Ekô* (transfer of merit).

In China, Buddhist monks who made it their business entirely to perform ceremonies were fostered together with the practicing monks who sought enlightenment. About the middle of the fifth century Emperor Wen Ch'eng of the Northern Wei dynasty erected the stone Buddhas of Yun Kang for the sake of commemorating the previous emperor. It is thought that the Emperors and the nobles before this also had entrusted to the Buddhist monks the performance of offerings for the dead. In the T'ang period sumptuous, esoteric ceremonies and forms were imported and influenced the mode of ceremonies for the dead. However, since the Chinese highly valued the funeral ceremonies carried out since the time of their ancestors, the Buddhist funeral rites did not become universal for a long time. It was probably after the Sung period that they reached the people. Particularly the Indian method of cremation did not please the Chinese who considered the dead body as important.

In Japan Buddhist funeral rites were performed at a comparatively early time. In the year 700 Dôshô is said to be the first example of one being cremated according to his dying request, but very early also Emperors such as Jitô in 703, Mommu in 707, Gemmyô in 721 and Genshô in 748, were cremated. Later, in the Edo period national scholars and Confucianists frequently criticized cremation when they attacked Buddhism.

The practice of cremation was spread among the people by the activities of *hijiri* (sage) and *shônin* (holy priest). It is said that Kûya who traveled the several provinces in the tenth century cremated the corpses discarded on the road, while reciting the name of *Amida Buddha*. Besides him, there were other such religious leaders. Thus together with the *Nembutsu* faith Buddhist funeral rites spread among the people, and after

the Kamakura period established the basis on which the religious sects of
the Pure Land lineage developed.

The offerings made after death are on the seven-seven day (i.e. forty-
nineth day), hundredth day, one full year, three full years, the thirteenth
death anniversary and the thirty-third death anniversary. These are of
Japanese character. However, they were not determined at one time, but
gradually increased their number. They were all present together about
the end of the Kamakura period.

In common with most of the people of the world the fiftieth or hundredth day at first generally marked off the period when the dead body,
which had been buried, decomposed and no longer retained its original
form. Next, when the period is as long as thirty years, it is because the
successors have reached old age and the nostalgia for those gone before
fades among people of the world. In such cases, the forty-ninth day,
hundredth day and thirty-third year anniversaries of the dead also have
anthropological explanation. But at the same time, the forty-ninth day
anniversary also has an explanation in Buddhist doctrine.

In the ancient sects of Buddhism in India there was the question
whether a man was born into the next life immediately, or whether he
remained in an intermediate provisional state [called in Japanese *Chûu*
or *Chûin*, (*anatarābhava*)] and its existence or non-existence was dis-
cussed. Generally the conservative sects affirmed the existence of *Chûin*,
and the progressive sects denied it. Even among those who affirmed the
Chûin period there were differences of opinion concerning its length
from a very short time of seven days to a very long time of forty-nine
days. This, so to speak, is a doctrinal problem, but in later ages the problem of rites for the dead were related to it. Since one's destiny was not
yet determined during *Chûin*, one had to carry out special rites during
that time. From such cases the seven-seven, forty-ninth day system of
offerings probably began.

It is said that in respect to the thirteenth year mourning period, it was
first done when Shônagon-nyûdô Fujiwara Shinzei's (d. 1159) sons
gathered for his sake on the basis of the fact that the twelve branches,
which are names of years in the duodecimal Chinese calendar system,

had completed a cycle and returned again to the first branch, making thirteen years. The thirty-third year mourning period began in the Kamakura period and the twenty-fifth in the Muromachi period.

The custom in which the dead spirit visits the home of his descendants at a determined time existed in ancient times. It is generally known that what we call *Bon* is an abbreviation of the Buddhist term *Urabon-e*, but recently, according to the theories of the ethnologists, a word was employed in ancient times called *Boni* differing from that. Whatever the name, speaking from its content *Bon* is a remembrance of a faith peculiar to the Japanese which existed before the arrival of Buddhism. Together with New Years, July was a special festival month. There is even today the custom of catching fish for one's living parent and of worshipping the spirits of the dead and the ancestors. Such ancient activities were later associated with Buddhism, and it came about that a *Bon* shelf was provided, and offerings were made to the ancestral spirits together with those who had died with no one to care for their spirits. The *Tanagyô* or Shelf Sutra, which one invited Buddhist priests to read, became universal, and in the Edo period, because of conversions to Christianity, this practice had the import of an inspection of the *Butsudan* (Buddha altar in the home). However, as we related before, its psychological foundation lies in the peculiar Japanese way of thought of the visit of the spirits of the ancestors to the home of its descendants at a particular time.

The Buddhist *Urabon-e* which is carried out in Japan was first performed by Emperor Wu ti of Liao dynasty in 538 in China, and it spread from about the beginning of T'ang dynasty. In Japan the first example appears in 657, the third year of the reign of Emperor Saimei.

As the authority for the Indian origin of this *Urabon-e* festival there is one volume in two translations called *Urabon-kyô* (Skt. *Ullambana Sutra*). According to it, the Buddha's disciple, Mokuren (Skt. Maudgalyāyana), saw that his mother was born as a hungry ghost and thirsted for food and drink. According to the Buddha's instruction, he offered food for the sake of his dead mother and father in the present generation and up to seven generations on the fifteenth day of the seventh month. He invited many monks and held a religious service. There is suspicion that the sutra was forged, and it can be inferred that it was probably compiled in China. However, it has been considered basic until the present time as the only literature which proves the Indian origin of the *Urabon-e* festival.

According to reliable literature, there is no proof that the *Urabon-e* festival was carried out in the Indian Buddhist Order, but there were similar beliefs in Indian popular lore. Probably such a popular belief was transmitted to China together with Buddhism. There it took a Chinese form and, later, coming to Japan, it combined with customs peculiar to that country.

With respect to the Indian popular belief, there is the following legend in the great historical poem, the *Mahābhārata*:

> A long time ago there lived a great ascetic named Jaratkāru. He traveled through the world and practiced his austerities living only on air. One day when he attempted to peer down a deep hole, there the spirits were hung with their heads down. As he looked, rats were gnawing the single rope on which they hung, and it appeared that at any moment they would cut it. As he watched such a pitiful situation, the ascetic inquired of those near him: "Why are you hanging in this manner?" They answered him, saying, "We have run out of descendants, and therefore we are suffering in this way. We had a son named Jaratkāru, but he became an ascetic and would not marry and have children." Upon hearing this lament, Jaratkāru searched for a woman suitable to him and married. He had a son called Astīka. After he had fulfilled his duty to his ancestors, he ascended to heaven.

Thus it was thought in the general belief of India that those who had no male successors suffered after death. This popular belief became associated with Buddhism, and the Buddhist reformulation was probably the *Urabonkyô*. *Urabon* is from the Sanskrit term *ullambana*, but this can be viewed as a corruption for *avalambana*, the noun derived from the verb *avalambante* (hung) in Sanskrit, in the *Jaratkāru* legend which we have introduced above (according to Ikeda Chôtatsu). It is an interesting example in which, mediated by Buddhism, this Indian popular belief was transmitted to East Asia, and there combined with the popular beliefs.

Even today there is the *Segaki* ceremony (feeding hungry ghosts) carried out as an accessory to the *Urabon-e* festival, but originally it derived from a different source.

According to the general beliefs of ancient India, spirits of the dead who had met tragic deaths and brought disasters to living beings were called *Bhûta*. They desired blood, and prowling around at night, they would pollute the earth, trees, rivers and lakes and mountains. It was the custom to make offerings to the *Bhûta*. *Bhûta* are also known as *Preta*, but these, having no descendants, do not receive offerings after death. Hence, they wander about human dwellings, and on occasion enter into dead bodies or take possession of the body of a sleeping person and do evil things. In Buddhist texts the *Preta* are called *Gaki* (hungry ghosts). In Buddhism an ethical significance has been added to it, and those who have done evil in their lives or were greedy were reborn as hungry ghosts after death. They always suffered from starvation. The *Preta* appear in various books common to Hinayana and Mahayana, and they are widely known in China and Japan as one of the six paths in the world of transmigration (hell, *Preta*, beasts, demons, man, gods). After the Fujiwara era, they stirred the imagination of the people with their fearful sense of reality in such works as folding screens, *kakemono* and picture scrolls which were called *gakizôshi* (stories of hungry ghosts). Today the two volume picture scrolls which are traditionally believed to be from the pen of Tosa Mitsunaga are famous.

Since the *Gaki* cannot obtain food and drink by ordinary means, it is said that the monks, when they ate, would provide food especially for them. This offering of food, that is, *Segaki*, feeding the hungry ghosts, came to flourish particularly in the *Mikkyô* school. Beginning with Kûkai, the monks of the *Mikkyô* school imported the rite of *Segaki*, and the devotees made it their business to perform this ceremony every night. From the Kamakura period most sects such as the *Zen* sect also performed it. And in the ninth month of 1422 the monks of five temples carried out a great *Segaki* ceremony at Gojô Kawara in Kyoto. Excepting *Jôdo Shinshû*, it came to be performed by all sects, and today most perform it on the occasion of the *Urabon-e* festival in July. It also has as its object those who have died in great disasters such as drowning, fire or earthquake.

The psychological basis of the *Segaki* ceremony is to offer food to the angry spirits who have been abandoned so that they do not do injury to living people, and, at the same time, to request that they should not act violently with the food which has been provided for the ancestors. Such a mode of thought existed among the Japanese before the arrival of Buddhism, and it was given a more formal arrangement by Buddhism. Observing this example, we can understand that the Buddhist form of faith in Japan was constructed on already existing concepts peculiar to the people.

The festival of *Higan* which occurs in the Spring and Autumn seasons has no certain, previous example in either India or China. It appears to have begun in Japan in the Heian period. It is recorded that for the sake of Prince Sawara who died a tragic death in the year 860 "the monks of the various provincial temples were caused to read the *Kongôhannyakyô* (Skt. *Vajracchedikā-prajñā-pāramitā Sūtra*) in the two middle months of Spring and Autumn (second and eighth months) for seven days." In the *Engishiki* (A.D. 927) also it is recorded that they had this sutra read for a week in Spring and Autumn and gave alms to the priests.

In the life of the Heian aristocrats *Higan* was a kind of feast day:

> It was sometime after the tenth of the second month, . . . as it is generally said, when it is the (time of) *Higan*: "We shall purify ourselves more than usual," and he had (his disciple) exchange his ordinary mat (where he prays) for a clean one. (*Kagerô Nikki* or *Diary of Dragon-fly*.)

> It was about the first day of the second month. The sixteenth day of the month being the first day of *Higan*, it was a very good day (*Genji Monogatari* or *Tales of Genji*, Chapter *Miyuki*.)

> He secluded himself for a short while in Kiyomizu . . . but because it was the time of *Higan*, it (the temple) was extremely bustling, and he went to sleep feeling terrible . . . (*Sarashina Nikki* or *Diary of Sarashina*.)

In the Kamakura period there was a ceremony called *Higan Sembô* (Repentance) and together with inviting the priests and lay people, a proclamation was made to the effect that "during the releasing of the birds in the *Higan* festivals of the two seasons, in the Eastern provinces killing is prohibited as well as hunting by burning fields and fishing by poisoning rivers and lakes." (*Azuma Kagami* vol. 8.) We may recall that when Christianity began to be transmitted to the German people, at Christmas time hunting was prohibited.

In the Tokugawa period *Higan* became a ceremony of the masses and temples also provided entertainments. In Edo there was the *Rokuamida-mairi* (pilgrimage to the six temples where images of Amida are enshrined) and in Osaka the Shitennôji temple was particularly popular. *Hakamairi* (visits to the cemetery) was universally performed, and the custom flourished of making *dango* (dumplings) and *botamochi* (glutinous rice and bean paste) and dedicating them before the Buddha. Then they were given to neighborhood people and friends. After 1879 the Spring and Autumn ceremonies were dedicated to the spirits of the Imperial house. Since the defeat in war in 1945, they have become days of the Vernal and Autumnal equinoxes. But the fact that they are days on which the ancestors are venerated has not changed.

At present when a person dies he is given a special name called *hômyô* or *kaimyô* (Buddhist posthumous name). It was the practice in Chinese and Japanese Buddhism to give a Buddhist name as a sign that one had entered the Buddhist faith. In the Tokugawa period it became the general practice to affix the special name the first thing after one has died. It came about that in relation to the inquisition of Christians, when one died, his funeral had to be carried out in Buddhist rites. This custom has continued to the present time.

The mortuary tablet (*ihai*) which recorded the Buddhist name was used since Kamakura times. It appears however that it was disseminated through the influence of Christian conversion. Originally ancient Japanese called it *yorishiro* or *tamashiro* (symbol of soul). This developed from what was thought to be the dwelling place of the ancestral spirit. However there was also influence from the tablets of the Confucian lineage, and they also appear to have imitated the style of the *Zen* school of the Sung period. The Buddha shelf (*butsudan*) as the place where the *ihai* are placed came to be provided generally in the home in the Edo period. However, *Jôdo Shinshû* believers did not forget that the *butsudan* in the original sense was the place where *Amida Buddha* was worshipped.

As we related before, the practice of making a grave marker by piling dirt on the place where the dead person was buried and placing a stone on it had already begun in the Yayoi period in the practice of marking the grave by constructing the form of a *stupa* from stone. Originally *stupas* were constructed in India, and Buddha's remains were gathered in them. This was also the origin of the *stupas-pagodas* in China and Japan. Since the Kamakura period it came about that monuments were erected on which the names were carved on a stone slab called *itabi* or *hanbi*. From that various types of tombstones have developed.

Among the tombstones was the five storied pagoda in which, from the bottom, five stones were piled in the order of shape, square, round, triangular, semi-circular, and jeweled, symbolizing the five great elements of earth, water, fire, wind and space. On them were carved the Sanskrit letters corresponding to the sounds: A Va, Ra, Ha, Kha. It was originally a symbol of *Mahāvairocana Buddha* (*Dainichinyorai*), the *Dharmakāya* (Law Body of the Buddha), but later it was used generally as a tomb marker. When it is carved on a wooden post it is called *kakutôba* and when it is made on a long slender block of wood it is called *tôba*, and it is set up in the graveyard in order to memorialize a dead person. The terms *tô* and *tôba* are transformations of the Sanskrit word *stupa* which originally was a Buddhist landmark where remains of the Buddha were consigned. Nevertheless, it is a practice peculiar to Japan that these simplified forms came to be used in rites for the dead.

It is a Japanese way of thought that a dead person is generally called *Hotoke* (Buddha). There is a problem concerning the derivation of the Japanese word *Hotoke*, but it is certain that it corresponds to the Sanskrit *Buddha* and the Chinese expression *Fu t'o*. There does not exist in Buddhist thought the idea that all men become Buddhas when they die. Since Buddhahood is a state in which a man has realized his ideal, there is no reason that one can say that just because he dies, he becomes Buddha. Since this also comes from the Japanese way of thinking, as we related before, a man, when a specific period of time passes after death, becomes an ancestral spirit and is called *Kami*. This word *Kami* was replaced by *Hotoke* in our present manner of speaking. Even though the word is Buddhist, the content is folk belief itself. The term *Jôbutsu* (to become Buddha) also does not have the meaning to become Buddha, but is nothing more than to say that the unstable, dangerous dead spirit is pacified on becoming an ancestral spirit. In the case of angry spirits, it is necessary to hold special religious rites in order to have them "become Buddhas." From such a situation, rites for the dead clothed with Buddhism have developed in Japan on the foundation of folk belief.

That the performance of ceremonies for the dead was not the original function of Buddhist priests, everyone is aware. Further, it was inconceivable that they would perform these as their profession. Here we shall quote a word of Shinran:

> I, Shinran, have never once said the *Nembutsu* for the sake of filial piety to my mother and father. The reason is that all beings together are mother and father and brothers through ages and births. Each will save (others) by becoming Buddha in the next life. I may not save my mother and father by transferring (the merit of) my *Nembutsu* even though it is a good deed which I do on my own power. Only if we quickly attain the enlightenment of the Pure Land by rejecting self-power can we save those to whom we are related, first of all, through divine means, even stilling all the karmic suffering in the six paths and four births. (*Tan'i-shô*).

The immediate problem here is that one cannot recite the *Nembutsu* even for the repose of the souls of one's own mother and father. One must first reject the self power and attain enlightenment by pure Other Power. After that we may say that we shall save those with whom we are familiar. Consequently, in our present standpoint, it is obvious that we cannot guide the dead.

Further Dôgen has stated thus:

> The masses on mourning days and the good deeds done during *Chûin* (the seven weeks' mourning) are all employed by laymen. Zen priests must truly be aware of their deep gratitude to their parents. All my deeds should be like this. Do you suppose it is the Buddha's idea to practice prayer just on a special day to special people? (*Shôbôgenzô-zuimonki*, No. 2.)

We observe in this that it was the practice in the general society of
that time to do good acts for the repose of the parents' souls. According
to Dôgen, of course, those who have left home as monks do not forget
the obligation they have to their parents, but it does not comply with
the Buddha's idea to transfer merit on a special day for only definite
people. When they held the thirteenth year memorial service for Shô-
nagon Nyûdô Shinzei, which we related above, Myôhen, who was one
of his sons, said that because he had become a *Nembutsu* devotee and
retired to Kôyasan he refused to participate. This was a period earlier
than either Shinran or Dôgen. When we put these together it appears
that monks in their original sense did not participate even in the services
for parents.

From ancient times Buddhist priests performed prayers and funeral
ceremonies for the Emperors and nobles. However, the various sects of
the older Buddhism did not have to request a charge for the funeral rites.
But from the Kamakura period new conditions developed. The newly
arisen sects, particularly the monks of the Pure Land lineage which did
not have the protection of the nobles or income from real estate, appeared. They could not expect income at all through prayers because of
their stand in rejecting the principle of benefits in this life (*genze riyaku*).
The only way left to them was a charge for funeral services. This also
was not an easy way at first but, since the way was prepared through the
travels in the regions of the *hijiri* (sages) and *shônin* (holy priests), it was
convenient to employ the thought of rebirth in the Pure Land as an
explanation for the funeral rites. Thus the parish relationship was first
established in the organization of the Pure Land line (*Jôdo*), and temples
developed which had funeral rites as their chief source of income.

When once this form materialized, other sects also imitated it. The
Zen temples in the various regions, as we noted before traced a course
from places for practice of *Zazen* (sitting and meditating) to places of
prayer (*gokitôsho*) to the family temple (*bodaisho*). The older sects such
as *Tendai* and *Shingon* also could do no other than to travel the same
path, because of the collapse of the nobility which had been their pro-
tector, and the pillage and destruction of their real estate by the warriors.

Hence, in the period until the later feudal system was established, the greater part of the temples, without distinction as to doctrine, had funeral rites as their main function or prayer their business. It was not uncommon that they combined both. Although the Tokugawa policy stabilized the temple-parish relationship and brought about the inertia of Buddhism in Japan, the way had already been prepared for this long period.

It is clear that funeral services were not the work of monks in Śākyamuni's Order. They were the task of the hereditary Brahmins. In East Asia such was not the case. When Buddhism came to act as agent for the folk religion, it became responsible even for funeral rites.

When Śākyamuni was still a prince, he saw an aged person, a sick person, a corpse and a mendicant, and this became the occasion of his leaving home and taking up austerities. The problem of life and death was the occasion for considering the religious problem seriously. "To consider life and to consider death is the one important cause and condition of a Buddhist." (Dôgen) To grasp life and death clearly is extremely important. In Japan, through the formalization of funeral rites, Buddhism has gone so far as to lose sight of the serious pursuit concerning life and death. If one considers that Buddhism has a living road in the future, there is probably nothing else to do but to advance in the direction of rejecting the cloak of funeral rites which is satisfied with mere form, and both to have confidence itself concerning life and death and to indicate it to others.

Opposition and Compromise

When a powerful foreign religion is newly imported, the former folk religions oppose it, or are destroyed, or they transform and unite with it. When Christianity was propagated in Western Europe, the folk religions were usually destroyed, but most of their essential elements were transformed and lived on in Christianity.

Even in Japan, Buddhism experienced a number of stages in development. From the very beginning of its importation, there was no great

opposition. The author of the *Nihon Shoki* (A.D. 720) has noted concerning the Emperor Yômei: "The Emperor believes in the Buddhist
Dharma and reveres Shinto." In such a way it was very common to believe in Buddhism and Shintoism together. In the year 676, on the
occasion of a great drought, there is a clear example in which "messen-
gers were sent in the four directions and prayers were made to the deities
of heaven by dedicating Shinto offerings, and further all the monks and
nuns dedicating Shinto offerings, and further all the monks and nuns
were requested to pray for the three treasures (*tri-ratna*)." As this indicates, it was reliance on the gods in a terrible time, and they made prayers
to both the Shinto gods and Buddhas without distinction as the occasion
demanded. Even today in the usual house the Shinto shelf and the
Buddha altar are worshipped side by side and Japanese participate alike
in services of Shinto shrines and Buddhist temples. Such is the general
Japanese custom. This Japanese practice which may seem strange when
viewed from the standpoint of monotheism was also probably carried
out without any sense of strangeness from the beginning of the arrival
of Buddhism. Of course, the question did arise as to the relation of these
religions which had differing lineages. However, it almost never developed to a profound religious conflict such as we see in other countries.

Buddhism, on its part, generally recognized the existence of the gods
peculiar to Japan and in some form attempted to accommodate and unite
with them. There were a number of stages in this process.

Setting aside the simple way of thinking which prays to either gods
or Buddhas without reflection, we see in Buddhist sutras that the Indian
gods (called *shoten*, Skt. *deva*) served the Buddha and played the role of
defenders and protectors of Buddhism. In Japan also, Buddhism, on its
part, recognized the gods of Japan as the protecting deities of Buddhism.
For example, on the occasion of the construction of Tôdaiji temple in
749 in an oracle of the Usa *Hachiman Daijin* of Buzen province, aid in
the completion of the work was promised:

> I will certainly perform this, leading the gods of heaven and earth. It
> is nothing special. Molten copper shall flow like water, and my body

mixed with grass, wood and earth, I will achieve this without much trouble.

There are many examples later of the thought of Buddhist protecting deities. In 804 when Saichô went over to T'ang China the god of Jin-gûji temple of Kahara appeared and announced:

> I am the God of Kaharu. I beseech you that you are fortunately immersed in the great sea of the Compassionate Vow. Please save quickly those people suffering in the way of Karma. I will assist those who seek the *Dharma* and protect them day and night.

When Saichô built the Enryakuji temple on Mount Hiei he worshipped the god *Ômiwa*. When Kûkai opened Kôyasan it is said that there was an oracle from the goddess *Nibutsuhime Myôjin* to the effect:

> I have been seeking happiness in the way of Shinto for a long time. Then the Bodhisattva (Kûkai) came to this mountain. The disciple (myself) is fortunate. I express my faith by giving you my garden (Kôyasan).

The idea that the gods are tutelary deities of Buddhism remains even in later ages. However a way of thought which was not content with that belief appeared in the middle of the Heian period.

In the second stage the gods were recognized as originally the same as Buddha. The gods were originally Buddhas themselves and they were manifested in Japan as the gods.

A concept similar to this had already appeared in India also. In Hinduism, for instance, the god *Vishnu* was believed to appear on earth in different forms at different times. This manifestation was called *Avatāra* (Jap. *Gonge*). Śākyamuni died at the end of a lifetime of eighty years but that was only a temporary form. Buddha's original body (essence), the *Dharma-kāya* (Jap. *Hosshin*, the "Truth-body") is eternal. This mode of thought appears in many sutras. In the chapter on the Eternity of the Tathāgata of the *Hokekyô*, it is stated:

> It is a great eternity since I have become Buddha. My life is infinite aeons and it is eternally indestructible.

This probably had a great influence on Japanese Buddhism. Thus the mode of thought was established that the gods of Japan were the manifestation of the form of the Buddha who is an eternal existence.

In the third stage, individual gods came to be analyzed into manifestations of special Buddhas and Bodhisattvas respectively. The original Buddhas or Bodhisattvas were called *Honji* (the original) and the form as a god, *Suijaku* (manifestation). It is the theory of *Honji-suijaku*. For instance, such examples as *Hachiman* as the manifestation of *Tathāgata* of Infinite life (*Amida-Amitābha*) and *Kumano Sanjo* as the body of *Ise Daijingû* which is the manifestation of the *Kuse Kannon* (*Avalokiteśvara*) can be seen from about the beginning of the twelfth century. In 1164 when Taira Kiyomori dedicated a copy of the *Hokekyô* to the Itsukushima Shrine, it is recorded on the text of petition (*Gammon*): "The (deity) of this shrine is a manifestation of *Kuse Kannon* (*Avalokitesvara*)." Examples of this become more frequent in the Kamakura period.

As the national thought became stronger a mode of thought appeared as the fourth stage in which the gods of Japan were the *Honji* (the land of their origin) and the Buddhas were the *Suijaku* (manifestations). This idea came from about the fourteenth century. However, it was only a theory of one segment of thinkers of Shinto lineage. As an actual problem of faith, it had hardly any influence. It was in the Edo period that Shintoism was organized and came into conflict with Buddhism.

Let us observe here relations with other foreign thought. Confucianism which was transmitted from the continent along with Buddhism was adopted as a system of ethics and morals, theory of government or as general education more than as religion. Conflict between Buddhism and Confucianism also had to arise in later generations. In the Heian period, Confucian scholars often composed the Chinese texts for the Buddhist services.

Similarly various folk beliefs were transmitted from the continent. What we call in one word Taoism contained besides the philosophy of Lao tzu and Chuang tzu, the teaching of *Yin-Yang* which contains folk beliefs, magic, astrology and fastings. In the time of the Suiko court (602) the Paikche monk Kanroku transmitted an almanac, a book of astronomy, geography and a book of sorcery, and consequently, for the first time three or four men were chosen and permitted to study. The teaching of Yin-Yang (Onyôdô) was investigated throughout the Nara and Heian periods, and it was responsible for astronomy and the calendar. From about the middle of Heian the magical aspect became more intense and with the decline of the nobility, it became the leader of popular magic. Further, many rituals which are carried on at the present time concerning auspicious days, directions in moving, one's fortune, compatibility (through divination), astrological rituals and "aspect divination" (hôi), began in the teaching of Yin-Yang. From the medieval period, excluding Jôdo Shinshû, it was frequently the case that the general run of Buddhist sects adopted these magical elements.

The thought of wizardry also is associated with Taoism and in such legends as that of En-no-Gyôja, it was assimilated to Buddhism. But, generally it did not go beyond hardly a literary interest. Even (the thought of) Lao tzu and Chuang tzu, which was the constituent element of Taoist theory, only seldom attained more than a scholarly interest.

However, the thought which is called Sangyô (three doctrines), in which Confucianism is political activity, Taoism is the life for recluses and Buddhism is asserted over against these two, was expressed in various forms. On the one hand, there was the interpretation of this theory which stated that the three teachings have respectively their own peculiar standpoints and are all excellent teachings and, on the other hand, there was the theory that for Buddhists there is no necessity to take notice of the other two doctrines.

To begin with, as a representative of the first standpoint, we see the teaching of Kûkai. In his work Sangôshiiki, which was his first published writing at the age of eighteen, he argued the excellence of loyalty and filial piety, the wizardry of the recluse and the Buddhist ideal concept of man. Finally he related the principles in which Buddhism ultimately was superior. In one passage of his preface we read:

> As I consider it, the nature of all things is not at all the same. As there is the bird which flies in the air, there is also the fish submerged in water. Hence, sages guide people by teaching the three of Buddhism, Taoism and Confucianism. There are differences of superficiality and profundity,

but all are the teachings of sages. Whatever among them one follows, it is not to be expected that he will act against loyalty and filial piety.

It was Nichiren who came close to Kûkai on the point that the three doctrines are a unity:

> There are three persons whom all persons should reverence. They are, so-called, ruler, teacher and parent. Further, there are three things which should be studied. They are Confucianism, non-Buddhist teaching and Buddhism. In Confucianism. . . . Lao tzu was the teacher of Confucius. . . . Secondly, the non-Buddhist teachings of India . . . are most important because the teachings of the non-Buddhist ways are an introduction to Buddhism. Thirdly, the great enlightened, World Honored One is the great teacher of all beings, the great eye, the great bridge, the great field of blessing. Even the words of the sages and saints in the non-Buddhist texts and ways are spoken without error, and their words and ideas mutually correspond. Still more the Buddha was a man who did not speak falsely from infinite kalpas. Thus the preaching of a lifetime of more than fifty years is a Great Vehicle (Mahayana), if we compare with the non-Buddhist texts and ways, and it must be the true word of great man. (*Kaimokushô*.)

The content is confused to some degree, but he explains Confucianism and Taoism as number one, non-Buddhist religions of India as number two and Buddhism as number three, and he recognizes the point that even categories one and two are the teachings of sages and saints.

However, on the other hand, there was also the method of asserting as far as possible, the purity of Buddhism and drawing a decisive line with other religions.

> O how sad it is that the priests and laymen
> Choose auspicious times and lucky days;
> While reverencing the gods of heaven and earth,
> They perform divination and Shinto ceremonies.

> O how sad it is nowadays,
> That the priests and laymen of Japan all together,
> Have Buddhist dignity (solemnity) as their basis,
> But they worship the spirits of heaven and earth.

The above are poems (*wasan* or hymns) of Shinran, and he lamented in this way the fact that non-Buddhist elements had become intermixed with Buddhism. This attitude of his was inherited by his successors. Because they make no pilgrimages to the shrines, they have been criticized by Japanese classical scholars. (It resembles the incident in which, during the Pacific war, Sophia University of Catholic connection collided with the Japanese military because it refused to make a pilgrimage to Yasukuni shrine.)

Dôgen, more keenly criticized the theory that the three teachings are in harmony:

> Further, slovenly persons say: "The highest reaches of Taoism, Confucianism and Buddhism must be all the same. It is only that for a while there are differences in the first steps." Or, they are likened to a three-legged kettle. These are the principles which now monks of the great Sung China discuss more eloquently. Speaking this way, those careless persons completely do away with Buddhism. We may say that they do not have so much as a speck of dust of Buddhism.

The intention to assert only pure Buddhism appears clearly in this passage, but since Dôgen's successors were not exclusive like the followers of Nichiren and Shinran, friction with other sects never arose.

In the Edo period the argument for the expulsion of Buddhism arose from both sides, the Confucianists and scholars of the National Classics and from the Shintoists. Among them the discussion of Hirata Atsutane stood on detailed research. We can say there were also many misinterpretations, and there were also many opinions rich in suggestions. In addition to the general stagnation of Buddhism, and the corruption of the monks in the Edo period, there were criticisms of Buddhism and the movement for the restoration of Imperial rule advanced in the direction of the persecution of Buddhism.

During the time from Meiji to today, together with the fact that Buddhism generally, on one hand, complied with the national policy of the time, it indicated a tendency to harmonize with Western European thought also. The argument with Christianity also in the Meiji period never attained to profundity. Most Buddhists during wartime complied with nationalism and after defeat in war manifested good will even with respect to American democracy and Christianity. However, Buddhists generally are compromising. What is the matter that there are many cases in which not only in respect to those outside Buddhism, but even toward those quasi-religious groups which develop within Buddhism a resolute attitude is not indicated? Do we view this also as a manifestation of the virtue of tolerance? Or, shall we call it a lack of vitality? Opinions will probably be divided on this.

Formalism

If taken in a certain sense, Japanese Buddhism is generally compromising, we can also say that it lacks seriousness. Japanese generally do not think seriously on the problem of religion, and it is not seldom also that they treat it playfully. In the sixteenth volume of the *Manyôshû* where playful songs are collected there is the following exchange:

> A song in which Ikeda-no Asomi ridicules Ômiwa-no Asomi Okimori:
>
> The female *Preta* of the temples say:
> If we are given the male *Preta*, Ômiwa,
> We will bear his son.
>
> The song of Ômiwa-no Asomi Okimori in which he ridicules in return:
>
> If you lack vermilion to make a Buddhist image,
> Then dig on the nose
> Of the puddling Ikeda-no Asomi.
>
> (What the female *Preta* in the temples are saying is that if they are given the male *Preta* Ômiwa for a husband, they would like to bear his son. They made fun of the fact that Ômiwa-no Okimori had gotten thin. If there was insufficient red for painting when making a Buddha-statue, it would be alright to dig around Ikedasan's nose. He said this because Ikeda-no-Asomi had a red nose.)

Particularly in the answering poem one feels a too sacrilegious spirit, but how is it?

Even in later generations when Buddhist priests appeared in such things as kabuki, for instance, it was frequent that people snickered and laughed. It appears that something humorous is associated with Buddhism.

It is perhaps from the Edo period that the temple pilgrimage lost its original meaning for faith, and became an excursion like a picnic. However, it appears that its origin was more ancient. It is the same for the Ise pilgrimage. For groups such as religious associations, going to shrines and Buddhist temples was a type of recreation trip. There were many light-hearted persons for whom faith came second to pleasure. It is not surprising that such immorality as drinking and prostitution was associated with it. (Even in Europe prostitutes haunt near the churches, it is said, but at least in modern times pleasure is not so openly associated with pilgrimages to churches as in Japan.) In recent years, instead of concealing the appearance of tawdry pleasures, the temples have frequently become places for sightseeing and have made the sightseers of famous places their partners. It is a poor substitute that such activity is distantly related to the true essence of religion.

That the Japanese, generally, when they contact temples and priests with such attitudes, do not attempt to discover an inner, fundamental religious experience, results from their concern with only the forms of religion. More than learning Buddhist doctrine and its ethical implications and attitude of life, they learned first to build temples, construct Buddha images and hold rituals. On the point that they have learned the form and externals of Buddhism, the Japanese have exhibited extraordinary ability. One may observe the art of Suiko, Hakuchô, Nara or the style of culture in the Muromachi and Azuchi-Momoyama periods. Many named and nameless geniuses, imitating and modifying Continental culture, produced superb works.

An empty formalism was dominant even in Buddhism, because of an imbalance in external form and content. For those who choose the Buddhist way of life, it is expected that adherence to the Buddhist standard of life—the precepts—emerges from an inner demand, but in Japan devotees were excessively scrupulous in external forms. The rite in which one vows to enter into the Buddhist way of life is that of receiving the precepts (*jukai*) and the place of the ritual is the precepts platform (*kaidan*). In Japan being recorded as a professional priest was "receiving the precepts" and the place of recording came to be called the "precepts platform." It was required that one observe the precepts more as a professional duty than by one's own desire. Consequently the precepts themselves became formalized.

The word *shôjin* originally meant effort or exertion, but in Japan it was necessary to exhibit it in concrete form. To live in a religious manner and particularly not to eat meat and fish came to be called *shôjin*. We observe that, since stories of monks who ate fish and poultry were frequently transmitted in medieval tales, it is difficult to restrain oneself from eating meat, and we can understand that those who refrained from it were reverenced.

In order to maintain the special privilege of the priest, celibacy and purity were required. To keep the body pure was considered necessary also for magical effectiveness.

It is recorded that there were many monks who married and had families from the beginning of Heian through the Kamakura periods, and it was not rare in Shinran's time. That Shinran married openly should be considered also in connection with the fact that he resolutely dissociated himself from magic. In teaching which has magic as its principle, by its nature priest's marriage is a difficulty.

Although after Meiji it was said that one might marry and eat meat at his convenience, most priests externally pretended to be celibate. Among those who claimed ability in magic and prayers, this tendency was especially strong. For that reason it appears that there were not a few illegitimate children.

When a religious body is formed on the basis of such formalism, a special priestly class comes into existence. In cases where there is a closed religious organization having hereditary temples as the main constituent, as in *Jôdo Shinshû*, it is obvious. In other sects in recent times the hereditary tendency has become increasingly strong. Besides that, with the formation of special societies through the old apprentice system, a religious group which we may also term a so-called caste has been constituted.

There never existed in Japan a religious reformation which was a first step toward modern society. In the newly arisen religious sects of the Kamakura period only one or two founders exhibited a freshness. Soon these sects became completely fixed and one wing of the feudal system. Even the *Shinshû* Order ultimately ended as one of the feudal powers. Finally, religious reformation as the womb of modern capitalism in the manner observed in Europe did not appear in Japan. Thus the premodern, formalistic religious bodies, still continue to exist today in Japan.

CHAPTER III

Establishment of Sects

In Japan it developed that all temples and priests belonged to some sect. There are also cases of a single independent temple being considered as a sect. Parishioners also belong to some temple, through which they become the parishioners of a specific sect. This is nothing more than the inertia of customs established in the Edo period.

Previously in India there never existed sects like those of Japan. Among the eighteen or twenty divisions of the Hinayana, there only were some differences in sutras and precepts, or differences of opinion in scholarly theory. They are something like sects within sects. Their distinctions were not such as one sees between *Shingon* and *Zen* sects or *Shinshû* and *Nichiren* sects. Sutras, precepts and rituals generally were the same in Indian sects.

While we speak of Hinayana and Mahayana, there was no distinction in India such as we consider in Japan. The monk I ching of T'ang China, who traveled in India for more than twenty years at the end of the seventh century, reported that "those who worship the Bodhisattvas and read the Mahayana sutras were Mahayanists, and those who did not were the Hinayanists." And I tsing himself studied the Hinayanists *Sarvāsti-vādin* precepts and transmitted them to China. Even though one might call himself a Mahayanist, at that time it was not because he had different precepts from the Hinayanist.

Further, according to the report of I tsing, in Mahayana there were two schools, the Middle View (Jap. *Chûgan*; Skt. *Mādhyamikavāda*) and Mind Only (Jap. *Yuishiki*; Skt. *Vijñānamātravāda-Yogācāra*). Only differences of opinion in philosophy distinguished these two schools. It is safe to say that in India there was no shadow of what are called sects in China and Japan. Then why did sects develop in China?

The first sect in China was the *Tendai* (Ch. *T'ien t'ai*) school of Chih i formed in the latter half of the sixth century. He arranged the sutras of holy writings (Jap. *kyô*) and those of doctrines (Jap. *ron*) with the Lotus Sutra (Jap. *Hokekyô*) which had already spread through China and established his own original system. Then he divided all Buddhist sutras into five categories and their modes of teaching into eight kinds. He asserted that the Lotus Sutra, as he understood it, was the pinnacle of Buddhist teaching. This method is called "Critical Classification of Doctrines" (Jap. *Kyôsôhanjaku*), but it is not based on objective historical research. It was only a subjective judgment boasting the superiority of his own sect. But it was necessary for him to devise a lineage of Indian tradition for his sect.

Following the *Tendai* school, in the T'ang era, the *Sanron* (Ch. *San Lun*), *Hossô* (*Fa Siang*), *Kegon* (*Hua Yen*) and *Shingon* (*Chen Yen*) schools were formed. In harmony with the movement for national unity, other groups also had to become established as sects. The various systems of *Vinaya* precepts (*Ritsu*), *Zen* and Pure Land (*Jôdo*) which had held freer views and activities had to be organized as sects. Even divisions made on the basis of research of such sects as *Bidon* (*Adhidharma*), *Jôjitsu* (*Satyasiddhi*), *Nehan* (*Nirvāna*), *Jiron* (*Daśabhūmika-śāstra*), *Shôron* (*Mahā-yāna-samgraha*), were traced back into the past and came to be treated as sects in the historical sense. Kumārajīva and Paramārtha were said to be men belonging respectively to the *Sanron* school and *Shôron* school, but this was actually a distorted view of the Chinese sects established in a later age. The structure called sect as a religious body was first constituted in the Sui and T'ang eras.

Sects did not actually exist in Japan at first. It is said that the priests Dôji, Chikô and Raikô were of the *Sanron* school, and Dôshô was of the *Hossô* school. Actually, however, they did not belong to specific sects. All they did was only to study those systems. Moreover, when we speak of the six schools of Nara, it is in the sense of branches of study generally and not sects which we speak of in later times. From the Heian period, stimulated by the formation of new sects, the *Hossô*, *Ritsu* and *Kegon* schools of Nara organized themselves in sectarian form.

We may say that the *Tendai* school of Saichô was the first sect to be established as a religious body in Japan. Saichô, who went to study in T'ang China in 804 and returned to Japan in the next year, first made an effort that Japanese Buddhism, including the older Buddhist sects of Nara, would be useful to the nation by becoming one body. Therefore, in the first month of 806 he sent a memorial to the Emperor and proposed that every year twelve monks chosen from all the sects be officially recognized. From the *Kegon*, *Tendai Hokke* and *Ritsu* schools, two persons each and *Sanron* and *Hossô* schools three persons each. Among the three one was to study *Jôjitsu* or *Kusha* school teachings. These monks were called "Yearly Monks" (*Nembundosha*). This system had existed previously, but Saichô tried to have the *Tendai Hokke* school, which he had newly begun, confirmed, and to ensure his successors. At the same time he tried to recognize the various sects of Nara on an equal basis and since both Nara and Kyoto agreed to this proposal, it quickly came into effect. With respect to the *Shingon* school, which was begun by Kûkai who returned to Japan a year later than Saichô, three "Yearly Monks" were allocated in 835. Later there were changes in the quota of persons, but generally the system was carried out until about the end of the tenth century.

To possess Yearly Monks was a sign that one's sect was officially recognized. Through this, the status of Saichô's *Tendai Hokke* school was acknowledged. However, in order for a young novice who had received his education on Mount Hiei to be conferred ordination, he had to go to the Nara ordination platform. The result was that though disciples were nurtured with great pains, it turned out that less than half remained on Mount Hiei. Accordingly, in 818 Saichô promulgated the *Daijôkai* (Mahayana Precepts), and he undertook the complete independence of *Tendai* even in the matter of precepts. Then at the end of a dispute with Nara, seven days after Saichô's death in 822, on the eleventh day of the sixth month, Imperial sanction was given for an ordination platform of

Mahayana precepts on Mount Hiei. By this the complete independence of Mount Hiei was realized and the status of the Japanese *Tendai* school became firm.

On one hand, Kûkai never came into conflict with Nara like Saichô and slowly but surely he constructed his status. In this way he finally made the *Shingon* school an established reality. The two great sects which were very powerful during the whole of the Heian era were thus created.

Each of the newly arisen sects of the Kamakura period strove for the public recognition of their existence as independent sects. It was so for the *Jôdoshû, Rinzaishû, Jôdo Shinshû* and *Nichirenshû*. Only Dôgen alone decisively refused to establish any denomination of his own.

Previously Śākyamuni had never been called a founder of a certain Buddhist sect. If what is termed a sect (*shû*) is the doctrine of Buddha, the founder, we would expect a previous example. Since there never was such a thing, those who advocate "sect" are not right. So Dôgen said. Since Dôgen followed the tradition of the "faithful transmission of the supreme truth of the Buddhist Ideal," he certainly, therefore, refused to call his group "*Zen* sect." Further, it certainly was not Dôgen's intention to call it "*Sôto* school." However, Dôgen's successors nevertheless came to advocate the sect name, accordingly as they became more powerful.

Opposition arose toward the new sects of the Kamakura period from Mount Hiei and Nara. Whenever the new sects tried to expand, the people of the older sects put pressure on the court and Shôgun, or they fought with the opposing sects directly.

Before this, the older sects, Enryakuji of Mount Hiei, Onjôji of Mii and Kôfukuji of Nara, each possessed monk soldiers, and from about the end of the tenth century they began to assert their power with violence. Nara was weakened through the oppression of Taira no Kiyomori, and the appeasement policy of Minamoto no Yoritomo, but Mount Hiei, up until the time when it was attacked and burned on account of Oda Nobunaga, used force by means of the military power of monk soldiers. On one hand, the newly arisen sects organized their followers and prepared military forces. The *Ikkô-ikki* (*Ikkô*-insurrections) of the *Jôdo Shin-*

shû school were very outstanding, and they wielded power in the area of Kinki (Osaka-Kyoto region), Hokuriku (Ishikawa-Toyama area), and Mikawa (Aichi region). Among these rebellions, the *Ikkô*-insurrection in Kaga province began in 1487, and in the following year the violence reached the extreme so that it was said: "The whole Kaga is an unruly province." In 1532 local lord Hosokawa Harumoto joined with followers of the *Nichiren* sect, which was very much at odds with the *Shinshû* school, and fought with the *Ikkô* party. Further in 1536 the warrior monks of Enryakuji temple fought with the *Nichiren* followers in Kyoto and burned their temples. They made a clean sweep of the power of the *Nichiren* sect from Kyoto. On that occasion, it is said that one third of the city of Kyoto was burned. Together with the advance of Oda Nobunaga's work of unifying the state, Mount Hiei was attacked and burned in 1571. Following the withdrawal of Kennyo of the *Ikkô* sect from the Ishiyama Castle in Osaka in 1580, General Toyotomi Hideyoshi destroyed Negoro in 1585 (Rf. p. 107) and forced the surrender of Kôyasan. Thereafter all the Buddhist temples were disarmed and certain ones were even eradicated. It may be said that there were almost none among the powerful temples of that time who were not included in the conflicts of military power. However, it should be noted that most of these conflicts were caused by struggles for secular power rather than by problems of belief.

General Hideyoshi supported the revival of the great temples which had once fallen into complete impotence or which were almost destroyed. The Tokugawa Shôgunate also inherited his policy and both protected the temples and supervised them. They determined strictly the sect-system so that the sects might not act freely. It came about that the system of registering monks, which had been relaxed since the medieval period, was revived, and the entire Buddhist Order was placed under national control. The sectarian organizations which remain until today were thus established.

In the sectarian system the great main temple (*daihonzan*) was the center and the branch temples (*matsuji*) throughout the country were under it. The priests, naturally, and also the parishioners, received super-

vision and control by the main temple. The main temple made an assess-
ment on the branch temples and safeguarded the advantages of the branch
temples. Sects had specific doctrines, but it was not always doctrine
alone which distinguished one sect from another. In not a few cases also
what we call independent sects arose because of a struggle for power. In
every age the political authorities have desired more to rule with the
great sects unified. It was true with the Meiji government and recently
at the time of the Pacific war the cabinet and military clique coerced
representatives of each sect and forced them unjustifiably to unite, per-
mitting them to continue to exist as a few great sects. For example the
Shingon sect which originally was divided into about ten sects was made
to unite into one group. After the defeat in war, the Religions' Division
of the General Headquarters, on the basis of religious freedom, enforced
a policy which permitted the free recognition of sectarian splits and
independence. It adopted the report system and stopped the older license
system. Therefore the condition of sectarian division and a flood of new
sects arose. According to the *Religions' Yearbook* of the Ministry of Education for 1963 the general number of Buddhist sects came to 170. According to the same statistics, the main lineages of the sects, their figures of
temples, teachers and parishioners are as follows:

	No. of Temples	Teachers	Parishioners
1. *Jôdo Shinshû*	21,609	33,603 (*1*)	13,093,692 (*2*)
2. *Sôtôshû*	14,892	28,241 (*2*)	9,971,723 (*4*)
3. *Shingonshû*	12,244	23,260 (*3*)	11,782,941 (*3*)
4. *Jôdoshû*	8,267	9,471 (*6*)	4,613,675 (*5*)
5. *Nichirenshû*	5,782	16,864 (*4*)	13,094,519 (*1*)
6. *Rinzaishû*	5,602	5,651 (*7*)	3,029,281 (*6*)
7. *Tendaishû*	4,383	14,206 (*5*)	2,929,948 (*7*)
8. *Ôbakushû*	479	450 (*11*)	162,077 (*9*)
9. *Jishû*	413	490 (*10*)	84,151 (*13*)
10. *Yûzûnembutsushû*	360	344 (*12*)	100,927 (*12*)
11. *Shingon Risshû*	84	99 (*14*)	117,270 (*11*)
12. *Hossôshû*	80	720 (*9*)	318,168 (*8*)
13. *Kegonshû*	57	736 (*8*)	68,181 (*14*)

14. *Risshû*	(24)	(56)(*15*)	(10,300)(*15*)
15. *Fukudenkai & Gedatsukô*	2	236 (*13*)	156,830 (*10*)

(As it stands on Dec. 31, 1962, except *Risshû*, the figures of which are those of 1956).

Looking at the above chart those which are the largest sects from the standpoint of numbers comprise one to seven. The order of the number of teachers aside from the top three is *Nichiren*, *Tendai*, *Jôdo* and *Rinzai* schools. The order in the number of parishioners is *Nichiren*, *Jôdo Shinshû*, *Shingon*, *Sôtô*, *Jôdo* and *Rinzai* schools. Sects in which the number of believers is greater in comparison to the temples and priests may be regarded generally as those in which evangelistic activity is vigorous. The four lineages of *Shinshû*, *Nichiren*, *Sôtô* and *Shingon* maintain a base of nine to thirteen million parishioners and decisively outdistance the others.

Among these, in both the *Shinshû* and *Nichiren* sects, the sectarian consciousness is strongest, and since the awareness of it is strong even in the parishioners, we may call them "closed sects" so to speak. Compared to these, we can call the other sects "open sects." There are many parishioners who are so only in form, and they are passive. There are also many for whom the points of faith are ambiguous.

Generally speaking, there has been a tendency for the sectarian consciousness to become gradually less, and persons concerned in each sect appear to be troubled by it. Actually, for a long time most priests were satisfied with being merely performers of religious ritual, and the parishioners, through national pressures, had become bound unwarrantedly to a specific temple or sect. Therefore, when the pressure was removed, it was natural that the union also would weaken. Especially, most recently, the newly arisen quasi-religions have taken advantage of this weak point, and they have vigorously laid waste the foundations of the sects of already existing religious bodies. We cannot expect to see great possibility that sects could continue to exist hereafter just as they were determined in the Edo period. At the present time the important factor which relates most Japanese to a Buddhist temple is that the graves of his ancestors are there. Their sectarian awareness is becoming weaker and weaker.

Considering the historical background of the various sects of Japan, we may classify them as follows:

1. *Ritsu* (Precepts). Excluding *Jôdo Shinshû*, a Buddhism without precepts is unthinkable. Here besides the *Ritsu* school we shall examine the movement for the revival of the precepts put forth by men in the *Shingon* and *Kegon* schools. In relation to that we shall also touch on the problem of the Mahayana precepts of Japanese *Tendai*.

2. *Zen* (Meditation). Meditation also is the fundamental practice for almost all Buddhist standpoints. Besides considering meditation in the Nara and Heian periods we will discuss also the *Rinzai* and *Sôtô* schools which flourished in the Kamakura period and the *Ôbaku Zen* which was imported from China in the Edo period.

3. *Mikkyô* (Esoterism). *Mikkyô* was known since the Nara period, but it flourished through the *Tendai* and *Shingon* sects of the Heian period.

4. *Kegon* (Avatamsaka School). The *Kegon* school, which was organized by Fa Tsang of the T'ang China and was based on the great literature called *Kegonkyô* (*Avatamsaka Sūtra*), flourished in the Nara period, and had great influence even on later ages.

5. *Hokke* (The Lotus of the True Law). The *Hokekyô* (*Saddharma-pundarīka-sūtra*) was widely disseminated in both China and Japan. It was especially prevalent in the Heian period scholastically as the *Tendai* doctrine organized by Chih i, and generally, in the form of magical faith in the *Hokekyô* itself. Nichiren constructed a new sect by means of faith in this text.

6. *Jôdo* (Pure Land). Among Pure Land beliefs particularly the faith that one attains rebirth in the Pure Land of bliss of *Amida* flourished from the Heian period. It developed, on the one hand, by the help of scholarly monks and, on the other hand, among popular religionists. In the Kamakura period three main sects were established, the *Jôdoshû, Jôdo Shinshû* and *Jishû*.

7. *Jôjitsu, Sanron* and *Hossô* schools. Even though they are important

for scholarship, they have little importance as sects, and we shall not touch on them here.

The Ritsu Lineage

In every Buddhist system, the precepts are fundamental. Precepts teach men who would try to realize Buddhist ideals what manner of living they must take and what standards of behavior they must observe (Rf. my *Bukkyô*, pp. 88 ff.). Since the ideals differ for monks who have left home and lay believers, there are also distinctions in the precepts to be observed by both, but when a person says that he is a believer in Buddhism, it is expected that he must observe the established precepts.

It is probably all right just to vow to the Buddha that one will keep the precepts (this is called *Tsûjujisei*, general reception of precepts by self-vow), but it is considered that the original rite was to perform the ceremony before a definite number of teachers and witnesses, and to make a vow to observe the itemized precepts (called Special Reception). In order to hold the ceremony, there are customs on detailed points and the place of the ritual. This reception of the precepts (ordination) is termed "conferring the precepts" from the side of the teacher and is also the rite for entering the Order. Frequently there were cases when it was viewed as a mere formality.

The text which records the provisions of the precepts, their derivation and the history of the order is called *Ritsu* (*Vinaya*), and every division had a different transmission. At present the *Pāli Vinaya* which is used in Southeast Asia is what was transmitted by the *Vibhajjavādin-Theravādins*. In Chinese also there exist several types of *Vinaya*, but among them the ones actually practiced are two, the *Shibunritsu* (Four Division *Vinaya*) of the *Dharmaguptavādin* and the *Jûjuritsu* (The Ten Recitation *Vinaya*) of the *Sarvāstivādin* group.

Among those (texts) of which there is no trace that they were practiced in India but were regarded as important in China, there was the *Bommôkyô* (*Brahmajāla-Sūtra*), particularly the second volume, *Bommô-bosatsukaikyô*. It is said to be a translation by Kumārajiva, but actually it was edited in China in the latter half of the fifth century, being based on Mahayana sutras and sastras. It was probably produced because Mahayanists were dissatisfied with only the Hinayana *Vinaya* which originated in India.

The *Ritsu* school in China generally had the *Shibunritsu* as its main constituent, and they interpreted it Mahayanistically referring to the *Bommôkyô*. The *Ritsu* school was also divided into three lines, but the one that was influential in later times was the *Nanzanshû* (Nan-Shan school of *Vinaya*) which was completed by Tao Süan in the T'ang era.

Zenshinni, who first entered the monastic life in Japan, received the precepts, when she studied abroad in Paekche of Corea and she returned to Japan in 590. From the reign of Temmu to the Tempyô period the *Nanzan* was transmitted. Dôsen (Tao hsuan) who came to Japan in 736 introduced both *Kegon* and *Ritsu* teachings. However, the fundamental transmission of the *Ritsu* school began with Kanshin or Ganjin (Chien chen) who came to Japan in the second month, 754. Because Chien chen came, an ordination platform was provided at Tôdaiji temple on the fourth month of that year and more than four hundred persons including the retired Emperor Shômu, Empress Dowager Kômyô, Emperor Kôken and the crown prince received the precepts. In the next year Kaidan'in (the Ordination Hall) of Tôdaiji temple was completed, and in 761, ordination platforms were provided at the Yakushiji temple in Shimotsuke (the Eastern Province) and at Kanzeonji temple in Tsukushi (Kyûshû). It turned out that the system of reception of the precepts was widely prevalent. Then in order to become a regular monk it was absolutely necessary to receive the precepts at the ordination platform. Consequently the Kaidan'in of Tôdaiji temple, not only in the Nara period, but also in the Heian era, preserved its prestige as the center of Buddhist authority. This was the system of precepts of the *Nanzan* school based on the *Shibunritsu* of Hinayana, but its interpretation and doctrine were based on Mahayana thought.

The system of the Kaidan'in was prone to become more formalistic rather than having inner significance in observing the precepts. Saichô who opened the *Tendai* school in the beginning of the Heian era at first

tried to cooperate with Nara, but they came into collision on the problem of ordinations. Finally, he resolved to construct an ordination platform for Mahayana precepts on Mount Hiei. We have related this in the
previous section. Saichô denounced the tradition of the *Ritsu* school as
Hinayana precepts, and he said that he would particularly advocate the
"complete and immediate" (*En-don*) precepts of the Mahayana. This
thought was by no means Saichô's own creation, but it was already in the
thought of his *Tendai* teacher in China, Tao sui. However, it was Saichô's own idea to say that he would construct an independent ordination
platform in order to offer Mahayana "complete and immediate" precepts, and this is peculiar to Japan. After Saichô's death the ordination
platform of Mount Hiei, which had been sanctioned by the court, prospered and produced many talented men. Hônen, the great leader of
Kamakura Buddhism, received the precepts on this ordination platform
at the age of fifteen, and Eisai and Dôgen both at the age of fourteen.
Among them, in the *Jôdo* school started by Hônen, the tendency was
strong to value the tradition of the precepts-receiving ordination, and it
developed into three lines. In the Edo period also there were those who
emphasized the *Endon* precepts. In this way the precepts of Mount Hiei
lineage have been transmitted also in the *Jôdo* school aside from the *Tendai* school. However, even after the ordination platform for the *Endon*
precepts was completed on Mount Hiei, the ordination platform of Nara
continued to prosper as a common place of ordination for many schools.
The *Shingon* sect also employed the Tôdaiji Kaidan'in for its traditional
Indian ordinations of *Gusoku* precepts.

The thought of precepts which had a deep Indian Buddhist coloring
appears not to have fitted the Japanese temperament. The *Nanzan Ritsu*
school, apart from the formal aspect of bestowing the precepts, was not
too active. In the Heian era also, the existence of the *Ritsu* school already
looked poorly. However, there were repeated movements to revive the
orthodox line of the *Ritsu* school.

In the Kamakura period there were several important figures in the
Ritsu school. There were many famous priests who excelled in precepts
and discipline beginning with Shunjô who went to Sung China in 1199

where for twelve years he studied *Tendai, Mikkyô, Zen* and *Ritsu*, and on his return to Japan revived the Sen'yûji temple in Kyoto. There were also Eizon and Ninshô (Rf. p. 19). Eizon revived the *Shibunritsu.* This line was called *Nankyôritsu* (Nara *Vinaya*) and had Saidaiji temple of Nara as its center.

Later during the period of civil wars it was not very active, but in the seventeenth century the *Nankyôritsu* (Nara *Vinaya*) was revived by men of the *Shingon* sect. The pioneer was Myônin who gathered persons of the same mind and ordained himself and made vows in 1602 at Kôzanji temple at Mount Togano-o in Kyoto. Thus the *Shingon Ritsu* school was established. He tried to follow the example of Eizon, the founder of *Nankyôritsu* and made his basis the *Ritsu* of the *Sarvāstivādins.*

After that several devotees of *Shingon Ritsu* school appeared successively. The most noteworthy were Jôgon and Jiun Sonja Onko (Rf. p. 16) who advocated the precepts of the true *Dharma* (*Shôbôritsu*). Sonja Onkô studied materials widely and required of monks the genuine practice of the precepts.

In the same period, reflection on the precepts came to be a problem also in the *Tendai* sect. From the Muromachi period it was not very active in either the areas of scholarly research or practice of the precepts. In the Edo period, through the political ability of Tenkai, it advanced in the Kantô region, but it was not sufficiently systematized in content. At that time Myôryû transferred from *Zen* to *Tendai.* He studied the fundamental texts of *Tendai* and asserted that one should practice by combining the principle of the precepts-receiving ordination with the self-vow and the *Shibunritsu.* Since Saichô had proclaimed the abolition of the Hinayana precepts for the *Tendai* school and established the Mahayana "complete and immediate" precepts, Myôryû's assertion was clearly a reversal of the fundamental standpoint of the sect. Myôryû's disciple Reikû, inherited his doctrine, and he made the Anrakuin on Mount Hiei, his hall of precepts (*Ritsuin*). His line of precepts has been called *Anraku-ritsu.* Of course, opposition to this was brought forward from the orthodox branch, and there were repeated disputes. However, after 1772 the *Anrakuritsu* was openly practiced, and also many scholars appeared in this branch. Actually, even today, this thought possesses great influence in the *Tendai* school. In short, it is a problem whether one can solve the question of practice with the thought of the Mahayana sutras such as the *Hokekyô* and the *Bommôkyô* alone as the sole guiding principle, or whether one can, as an individual devotee, also study at the same time the provisions of the *Shibunritsu* which places high value on formality. It appears generally to be the main trend in Japanese Buddhism to say that if one is establishing only basic attitudes, there is no need to be a slave to detailed items of the precepts. This is not a problem of the *Tendai* school alone.

The precepts for the general monk were already extremely relaxed in the Edo period. They barely maintained even a surface appearance through the penal regulations determined by the Shôgunate. When the new government of Meiji declared that the clergy could eat meat and marry at convenience, it now became unnecessary for the priests to observe the precepts. Or, there are even those who argue that it is the pride of Japanese Buddhism not to make a problem of the precepts.

Is this good enough? Just before Śākyamuni died, his last injunction was that it was alright to discontinue detailed items of the precepts if his disciples so desired. Since the disciples did not know which would be best to dismiss, they decided to continue to observe them all. Consequently, it is a fact that it (the *Ritsu-Vinaya*) also contains items which cannot be observed when conditions in the world change. However, the fundamental point is the basic Buddhist principle *Shoakumakusa Shuzenbugyô* which means "to practice good deeds without doing bad ones." There is no Buddhism that is not accompanied by moral discipline. Just hearing the *Dharma* (*Mombô*) is not Buddhism.

The Zen Lineage

The method of religious discipline called *Yoga* has been known from ancient times in India. It aims at achieving a heightened consciousness and the unification of the spirit by assuming a tranquil posture and controlling the breath. It is meditation, contemplation and mystical intuition. It is also believed that at the same time that one elevates his spiritual power by these means, he also increases his physical strength and can perform wonders.

These methods were observed by most ascetics in the sixth century before the Christian era. Gautama, becoming a mendicant, at first learned *Yoga* from masters, and after that practiced austerities for a period of six years. However, he could not realize religious ideals in those ways, and finally abandoned the practice of austerities. Instead he meditated with legs crossed under a great tree in the vicinity of the Nairañjanā River whose water is pure, and as a result he became "Buddha", that is, one who awakened to the truth. When Buddha undertook to guide his disciples, he always exhorted them to practice *Yoga*, so in Buddhism the terms *Yoga, Dhyana* and *Samādhi* are all used generally with the same meaning. The Chinese character 禅 (Jap. *Zen*; Ch. *Chan*) or 禅定 (Jap. *Zenjô*; Ch. *Chan ting*; *ting* is a unification of spirit), which copied particularly the vocalization *Dhyāna*, came to be generally known in China and Japan.

Dhyāna together with the precepts is the basis of all Buddhist practice. Since it is unthinkable that there can be a Buddhism without *Dhyāna*, there also did not exist a group of Buddhists in India who advocated only *Dhyāna*.

In China from the first period when Buddhism was imported, *Dhyāna* was also known. Particularly about the beginning of the fourth century, Hui Yuan also, who established the *Pe Lien She* (*Byakurensha*—White Lotus Society, an association of the *Amitābha* believers) at Lu shan in Chiang nan (provinces of Kiangsu and Anhwei), was diligent also in *Dhyāna* (*Zen*) together with *Nembutsu* (*Nien fo*). In the same era Kumārajīva and Buddhabhadra translated sutras relating to *Dhyāna*.

However, in later ages what is called the *Chan* (*Zen*) school is a group which is said to have inherited the tradition of Bodhidharma who came to China about the year 520. It was the *Zen* monks of the Sung period who gave life to the Buddhist way of life in the Chinese climate and they perfected a method of discipline which conformed to that way of life.

Those who draw from the stream of Lin chi I hsüen, who is a disciple of a disciple of Pai chang Hui hai of the Southern Sung, are the later *Rinzai* school. Also, those who appeared in the line of Ching yuan Hsing szu of the Southern Sung, a disciple of the sixth patriarch, Hui nêng, were the *Sôtô* school of today. These two great divisions were transmitted also to Japan as representative of the *Zen* school. In 1127 the Northern Sung was destroyed in China, and the Southern Sung revived. In this confused period two great *Zen* monks appeared. These were Tai hui Tsung kao of *Rinzai* and Hung chih Ch'eng chüeh of the *Sôtô* school. Tsung kao's mode of *Zen* practice is called *Kannazen*. The character *Na* or *Wa* (話) is the *Kôan* (Ch. *Kung an*, a word or phrase insoluble by the intellect) and it means "*Zen* in which one arrives at penetrating completely the great enlightenment by investigating the given *Kôan*."

Hung chih's style of *Zen* is called *Mokushôzen* (*Zen* in which one is illumined through silence). It indicates that one experiences inwardly a state of absolute freedom by earnestly undertaking *Zazen* and pacifying the mind. Here the *Kôan* is unnecessary.

These two methods were established at the beginning of the twelfth century, and later they were transmitted to Japan. They are the standards for understanding *Zen*.

From the beginning of the time when Buddhism was first transmitted to Japan, *Zen* was also known. We have related before (p. 17) that Dôshô built a *Zen* hall in Gangôji temple. In the Tempyô period Tao hsuan visited Japan and taught the precepts and *Zen*. Before Saichô went to study abroad, he had learnt the northern school of *Zen*. But in T'ang China at Mount T'ien t'ai he studied the line called *Gozuzen* (named after the monk Gozu in China who was founder). Since the Japanese *Tendai* school combined the four elements, *Tendai, Mikkyô, Zen* and *Ritsu*, it is not by chance that such famous Zen priests like Eisai and Dôgen appeared later from those affiliated with Mount Hiei.

There were those who transmitted *Zen* in both the Nara and Heian periods, but the time was not ripe. It was Eisai who began the *Zen* sect for the first time in our country (Rf. p. 11). Opposition appeared from Mount Hiei, but in 1202 he founded and constructed the Kenninji temple in Kyoto. This was the rise of the *Rinzai* sect in our country. There were many men of ability among his disciples.

Later the *Rinzai* sect greatly flourished centering in Five Temples (*Gozan*) both in Kyoto and in Kamakura beginning with the coming to Japan of Sung monk Lan chi Tao lung in 1246 and the arrival of Wu hsüo, Tsou yuan and I shan I ning. Tsou yuan had great influence on Hôjô Tokimune. I ning was the teacher of Musô Soseki, and the so-called *Gozanbungaku* (literature of the Five Temples) developed from this line from which men of talent issued. Chôdensu and Sesshû also, who were famous as artists, were affiliates of the *Gozan* group.

Dôgen, who first studied in the school of Eisai, transmitted *Sôtô Zen* over against the *Rinzai* sect. Dôgen went abroad to study in Sung China, and he sought a good teacher whom he obtained in the ideal teacher Ju ching of Tien t'ung shan. Ju ching was of the same line as Hung Cheng hsueh, and he taught the way of *Shikantaza* (singly and earnestly to perform *Zazen*). Dôgen, different from other monks who studied abroad, returned to Japan in 1227 bringing as a gift only the experience he possessed in himself, and in 1244 he founded the Eiheiji temple. This was the beginning of the Japanese *Sôtô* sect. Dôgen, faithfully following the way of Ju ching who had drawn from the stream of Hung chih Cheng hsueh, taught the younger generation and published in Japanese, among other things, the *Shôbôgenzô*. Dôgen denied the standpoint of seeking enlightenment outside of (apart from) practice. He made it clear that the practice itself is enlightenment, and enlightenment does not exist apart from practice. A life of effort itself was the ideal. Thus he ended a full life of fifty-three years.

From the Muromachi period the *Rinzai* sect had the tendency to associate with a way of life with aristocratic flavor and to become a leisurely sport. The *Sôtô* sect spread in the provinces, and developed as a popular religion, but it gradually weakened. Thus at the beginning of the Edo period the *Zen* sect as a whole was not very active. About this time the arrival of *Zen* monks of the *Ôbaku* sect, who were exiled to our country and avoided the turmoil at the end of the Ming China and beginning of the Ching dynasties, brought a fresh atmosphere. The *Ôbaku* sect belongs to the lineage of the *Rinzai* sect, but in the Ming period it became flavored with *Nembutsu* practice and doctrine and made its own peculiar development.

The pilgrim Tao che Ch'ao yuan who came to Japan in 1651 stayed barely eight years and returned to his country, but while he lived in Nagasaki, he was continuously visited by *Rinzai* and *Sôtô Zen* monks. Bankei Yôtaku also, at the age of twenty-nine learned from Tao che. Bankei advocated *Fushôzen* which was a teaching easier for the masses to understand. It held that man possesses the mystic Buddha mind, which is innate and not acquired in his life. Really to what extent Tao che influenced him we do not know, but it is at least certain to the extent that Tao's teaching became a stimulus for him.

Yin yuan Lung ch'i (Rf. p. 9), who came to Japan three years later than Tao che founded Ôbakusan Manpukuji Temple in Uji in 1662 and made it the main temple of the *Ôbaku* sect. The *Ôbaku* sect did not become great from the standpoint of numbers, but it has come down until today preserving its own peculiar style. Tetsugen is one representative Japanese who became a pupil of Yin yuan (Rf. p. 20).

On the other hand, in this period Shidô Bunan from the side of the *Rinzai* school taught a popular *Zen*, and avoiding fame he passed a noble life. His disciple Dôkyô Etan retired to Iiyama in Shinano province and pursued an earnest *Zen* way of life. He was called *Shôjurôjin* (the old man of *Samādhi*). It was the monk Hakuin Ekaku who went into a new life under this man. As he taught the doctrine in simple words and trained many disciples, even till the present time persons in his line are most numerous in the *Zen* sect.

In the *Sôtô* sect also there arose a movement for revival in the seventeenth century which, by volunteer activity centering in Manzan Dôhaku, changed the bad effects of two hundred years and opened the way to new developments.

Even today, the greater number of *Zen* temples and monasteries, similar to other sects, have become places of mystic prayers and ceremonies for the dead, but on the reverse side, there are diligent seekers of the way and not a few who work hard at *Zen* as active Buddhist laymen. Particularly in recent times, it has come about that it increasingly attracts the attention of intellectuals as one universal system of thought.

The Line of Mikkyô

There are many examples of mysticism in every culture. Following a European way of speaking, it is the belief that there is the possibility of an inner and intuitive union between a man's mind and the fundamental principle of existence. This union is not ordinary existence and cognition, but it is a way of existence and cognition which transcends the ordinary. Consequently, since it was frequently transmitted only to specific disciples who were endowed with complete qualifications within a scholarly group, it was called *Mikkyô* or *Hikyô* (esoterism, secret teaching) and was distinguished from *Kenkyô*, exoteric teaching which was taught openly to the general public. Because mysticism and esoterism are in line with the deepest in human nature, it can be present also in primitive societies and also can be manifested as the result of thought which has reached the ultimate in intellectuality. In order to understand the significance of esoterism in Buddhism, it is best to keep in mind again what we have stated above.

In considering the history of Indian Buddhism, we must distinguish *Mikkyô* apart from Hinayana and Mahayana. Indeed, this is not a contradictory relationship at all. If we regard the follower of Mahayana as one who worships the Bodhisattvas and reads Mahayana sutras, we can say that the follower of *Mikkyô* is one who organizes a mystic circle called a *Mandala*, recites spells and performs mystic ceremonies (*Ssuhô*). In India, although they speak of *Mikkyô*, it did not organize a sect different from the exoteric teachings, but people who followed the Mahayana doctrines at the same time practiced esoteric rites. It was after the seventh century that *Mikkyô* came to the surface in India. It was not a single isolated sect, but it must be understood as a tendency within the broad Indian religious current.

Sacrifice is one form of religious rite but if one particularly emphasizes the aspect of fulfillment of desires, it is a kind of incantation. Vedic incantation can be classified in three types. They are: (1) Protective (*Sokusai*), which wards off sickness and other misfortunes; (2) Improvement (*Zôyaku*), which increases and advances happiness and prosperity, and (3) Exorcism (*Chôbuku*), which is to curse demons and sworn enemies. These terms themselves were adopted also in *Shingon Mikkyô*. The form of the hearth and the classification of its use very much resemble each other, too.

The Buddhism of Śākyamuni originally was not a religion which taught incantations. However, it could not reject in its entirety the religious conceptions and rituals which were generally prevalent in the society of that time. There is much material in Buddhist texts which also reflects the folk beliefs of the age.

As is clear in the Brahmin religious literature, the esoteric tendency developed in the path of the evolution of Hinduism. On the side of Buddhism, esoteric texts were produced in response to this tendency. In the elements of esoteric ceremony, there is much that derives from folk beliefs, but what constitutes the essential nature of esoterism is the inevitable conclusion of Buddhist thought. Mahayana Buddhism asserts that the real and the ideal, delusion and enlightenment, are essentially identical from the higher standpoint of the absolute. If we push this perspective further we arrive at the view that it never rejects our actual life, including the feelings and desires of our instinct, but, on the contrary, by giving life in the true sense to the whole, one realizes the ideal. This realization is said to be achieved through the *Yoga* devotee's symbolic religious ceremonies (Rf. my *Bukkyô*, pp. 174 ff.). This is *Mikkyô*.

The Mahayana philosophers, both the *Mādhyamika* and the *Vijñānavāda*, thought that one experienced the world of absolute wisdom only through mystical intuition and symbolic rituals, and mystic rites became prevalent using such things as *Mudrā* (indicating various symbolic forms by inter-twining the fingers of both hands), *Mandala*, *Mantra* and mystery.

Mikkyô texts were already known little by little from about the third century in China. There were also missionaries who captured the minds of the politicians through the use of incantation. About the sixth century various forms of *Mudrā*, *Mantra* and mysteries were known. Since the style of these foreign magical practices were suited to the Chinese way of belief also, they were welcomed by people high and low.

It was in the beginning of the eighth century, in the reign of Emperor Hsuan tsung of the T'ang dynasty, that genuine *Mikkyô* was transmitted to China. Sabhākarasimba, who arrived at Chang an in 716 from India by way of Central Asia, is known by his Chinese name as Shan wu wei. He translated the *Daibirushanajôbutsushinpenkajikyô* sutra. This is the basic text of the *Shingon* sect and is commonly known as *Dainichikyô*. The *Dainichikyôsho*, a commentary compiled by a disciple I hsing, is regarded as indispensable for understanding the sutra.

Four years later than Subhakarasimha, the monk Vajrabodhi came to China by way of the sea from the south. His Chinese name is Chin kang chih. He also translated many *Mikkyô* sutras and had the confidence of Emperor Hsuan tsung. A very active individual was Amoghavajra (Pu kung chin kang) who was a disciple of Vajrabodhi and came to Loyang in the same year. He worked for half a century for the sake of *Mikkyô*, and he served, before and after the period of the An lu shan rebellion, three Emperors, Hsuan tsung, Suan tsung and Tai tsung. He translated over eighty texts of *Mikkyô* sutras besides the *Kongôchôgyô*. His influence was very great.

Hui kuo of the Ching lung ssu temple in Chang an, one of Amogha-vajra's many disciples, not only bestowed the doctrine on Kûkai, the founder of Japanese *Shingon* sect, but also produced many men of talent from his followers. However, *Mikkyô*, which originally flourished through the patronage of the T'ang Emperors, received a great blow with the decline of the T'ang dynasty and especially by the persecution of Buddhism by Wu tsung in 845. Later, there were also those who translated and studied *Mikkyô* texts in the Sung period. However there was no similarity to the T'ang period. In the Yuan period, Lamaism flourished. Finally there was no opportunity for the *Mikkyô* of the T'ang period to revive, but until 1924 when our Gonda Raifu bestowed the consecration ceremony for transmitting the *Dharma* (*Denpô Kanjô*) in the Kai yuan ssu temple in Ch'ao Chou, the orthodox line of T'ang *Mikkyô* was only passed on in Japan.

Diverse prayers were performed because from the beginning in Japan they attracted strong interest in the magical efficacy of Buddhism. Already in the earlier Nara period *Mikkyô* texts and various practices were known. Before Saichô and Kûkai went to T'ang China, the *Dai-nichikyô* among others already had been transmitted.

Saichô who went to T'ang China in 804 received *Mikkyô* teaching from Shun hsiao in the Kai lung ssu temple in Yueh chou in Chekiang province. It is said that Shun hsiao was a disciple of I hsing. After Saichô returned to Japan, he established the *Tendai* school, but he valued highly *Mikkyô* doctrine. He assigned one of the two Yearly Monks (Rf. p. 88) to the study of *Mikkyô*. After Saichô both Ennin and Enchin went to T'ang China and studied *Mikkyô* and it came to flourish on Mount Hiei more than *Tendai* doctrine. We call this *Taimitsu* (*Tendai Mikkyô*) in contrast to *Tômitsu* (*Tôji Mikkyô*) of the *Shingon* sect. *Taimitsu* and *Tômitsu* competed with each other in the practice of incantations through the Heian period.

Kûkai who went to T'ang China at the same time as Saichô studied orthodox *Mikkyô* under Hui kuo in the Ching lung ssu temple in Chang an. After he returned to Japan, he established the *Shingon* sect. With *Mikkyô* as the highest truth, he considered that all other Buddhist teach-ings apart from it were exoteric teaching, that is, a preliminary stage to *Mikkyô* doctrine. It is a peculiarity of the *Shingon* sect to value the practical discipline (*jisô*) along with the theoretical doctrine (*kyôsô*). In the thought of Kûkai a pan-Buddhistic view of the world was beautifully harmonized with the mystic ceremonies based on it. And he employed his experience in guiding the people and for practical social work. However, many of his successors stuck only to non-essentials, and they frequently fell into the evil of mere magical operations.

After Kûkai, besides the Tôji temple in Kyoto which was the center of his activity, and the Kongôbuji temple on Mount Kôya which is the place where he died, *Mikkyô* prospered at the Ninnaji temple and the Daigoji temple in Kyoto. Kôyasan temporarily declined at the end of the tenth century, but after the beginning of the eleventh century, it revived. In the beginning of the twelfth century the priest Kakuban appeared, who studied the ancient traditions and revived the practical aspects. Later, being persecuted by the priests and parishioners of Mount Kôya, he removed to Negoro, but his achievement in reviving the practical aspects was great. Also Kakuban is worthy of note as a forerunner of *Nembutsu* thought in the Kamakura period by the fact that he taught faith in *Amida*. He taught that from the *Mikkyô* standpoint *Amida* was essentially identical in nature with *Dainichinyorai* (*Mahāvairocna*) and that there is no Buddha-body outside our own selves (*Koshin Amida*) and that there is no *Jôdo* (Pure Land) outside of this real world. Kakuban's influence was great. After the end of the thirteenth century, he was revered as the founder of the *Shingi-Shingon* sect. After Negorosan, the fundamental place for the practice of *Shingi-Shingon*, was destroyed by Toyotomi Hideyoshi, it divided into *Buzan* branch, which had as its central temple the Hasedera temple of Yamato, and the *Chizan* branch whose central temple is the Chishakuin in Yamashiro (now Kyoto). Both were distinguished for Buddhist studies throughout the Edo period. They are called "New Principle" (*Shingi*) in contrast to "Old Principle (*Kogi*) *Shingon* teaching. It was after the Meiji period also that the *Chizan* branch and the *Buzan* branch were recognized as independent sects.

We have related above the relation of *Shingon* and *Ritsu* (Rf. pp. 16). Presently, speaking of the number of temples, the Kôyasan *Shingon* sect is most numerous and the *Chizan* branch and *Buzan* branch follow. The *Daigo* branch, the *Omuro* branch (*Ninnaji*), the *Daikakuji* branch, the *Tôji* branch, the *Yamashina* branch and the *Senyûji* branch have their central temples in Kyoto, and have relations with the Imperial house. The Daigoji temple is also the main temple for the practice of *Shugendô* (method of attaining spiritual experience by practicing in the mountains). The *Shugendô* group is composed of mountain monks (ascetics) who make their aim discipline in the mountains, and they have been a recognized sect belonging to both *Shingon* and *Tendai* since the Heian era.

With the division of Shinto and Buddhism in the Meiji period, sectarian activity ceased, but later it was revived.

Mikkyô is the product of the highest reaches of philosophical thought, and examples also exist in such places as Greece. It is also in line with a primitive magical faith. Even in India, it was considered indispensable in the orthodox branch of *Mikkyô* to study Buddhist philosophy deeply before entering into it. Kûkai also taught that doctrine should be accompanied by practice. Doctrine which is not accompanied by practice is meaningless in *Mikkyô*, and practice which is not accompanied by doctrine is only superstition. The object in the esoteric perspective is to teach a person the way to experience high religious ideals by increasing the welfare of man's actual life. We may say that there is no practical significance in *Mikkyô* except to bring about the elevation of both the spiritual and material aspects of the life of the people, through the unity of doctrine and the practices as embodied in the activities of Kûkai's life. In the *Dainichikyô* we read: "*Bodhi* mind is the cause; Great Compassion is the foundation and 'practical activity' (*Hôben*-expediency) is the ideal." Also it says, "Wisdom (*Chie*) and Expediency (*Hôben*)." It is the principle of *Mikkyô* to make men happy by being based on the highest wisdom and the mind of infinite love and in close touch with their actual lives. Should one depart from this path, there is nothing else to call it but an evil way.

Kegon Thought

The *Kegon* (*Avatamsaka*) sutra was not only loved as a Buddhist scripture in China and Japan, but also as subject matter in literature and art. That is because it is a noble and beautiful symphony.

It appears that it was never compiled in India in the form which we call the *Kegon* sutra. Two sections of it, i.e., the *Jûjibon* and the *Nyûhokkaibon* were originally organized as independent sutras, and their Sanskrit texts also presently exist. We may view these two sections as completed around the second century.

The *Jûjibon* explains the process in which the *Bodhisatva's* divine wisdom develops and unfolds as a series of ten stages. In the first stage of joy he arouses joy and faith, and in the second stage of purification, he separates from the pollutions of the mind. Passing through the successive stages, he finally arrives at the tenth stage of the *Dharma* Cloud (*Dharmamegha*) where he approaches the wisdom of Buddha.

The *Nyûhokkaibon* has a plot in which a youth, Zenzaidôji, following the guidance of *Monju Bosatsu* (*Manjuśrī*, symbol of wisdom) visits in succession fifty-three people (according to the mode of counting, fifty-five) and receives the doctrine. Finally he comes before *Fugen Bodhisattva* (*Samantabhadra*, symbol of practical activity), and is taught concerning the Buddha's wisdom. Among the fifty-three persons there are Buddhist monks, Brahmins, lay believers, ascetics and various women. Each lives in his own country and bestows upon Zenzaidôji the instruction. It is a piece of Buddhist literature which can be compared with Dante's *Divine Comedy* and Bunyan's *Pilgrim's Progress*.

Besides the *Jûjibon* and *Nyûhokkaibon*, sutras with similar tendencies were compiled. The sum total of thirty-four (or thirty-nine) compositions all together are called the *Kegon* sutra. They appear to have been edited in the region of Khotan in Central Asia, but at the beginning of the fifth century a sixty volume book, and at the end of the seventh century an eighty volume book were translated into Chinese. A forty volume book which was translated at the end of the eighth century only corresponds to the *Nyûhokkaibon*.

When the translation of the eighty volume *Kegon* sutra was completed in 699, the ruler of that time, Tse t'ien Wu hou ordered Fa hsiang to lecture on it. With this as its occasion, a new school called the *Hua yen tsung* (*Kegonshû, Kegon* sect) was born. Therefore, from the standpoint of fact, Fa hsiang is the founder, but from the formal aspect, he has come to be called the third patriarch of the *Kegon* school.

The *Kegon* sutra, in its entirety, portrays the content of Buddha's self awareness from the standpoint of the Buddha himself. It teaches that the whole universe is the form of the Buddha and originally we, sentient beings, also are nothing other than Buddhas. The whole universe is formed completely through infinite relationships. Everything is interacting in absolute freedom. Śākyamuni, who appeared as a man, practiced austerities, and became Buddha, is none other than *Vairocana* Buddha, the substance (true form) of the Universe. Thus the system of *Kegon* philosophy was organized on the principle that "one is all, all is one."

After Fa hsiang, scholarly priests continued to appear in the *Kegon* school, and they produced many commentaries. When we come to the Sung period, the *Kegon* philosophy merged with Chinese thought and had great influence even on the new form of Confucian philosophy. Traces of influence have been recognized also in Chu hsi who was the representative man of Sung scholarship.

Kegon was quickly transmitted to our country. There is a record that the *Kegon* sutra was copied in 722, and in 736 Tao Hsuan of T'ang brought commentaries related to *Kegon*. Also Shinjô of Silla (Shiragi, S. E. Korea) lectured on the *Kegon* sutra at the request of Rôben in 740. Shinjô became the first patriarch of the Japanese *Kegon* school and Rôben was the second. The Tôdaiji temple of Nara, whose construction began in 743, was the main temple of the *Kegon* school, and *Vairocana* Buddha, who appears in the *Kegon* sutra, was enshrined in the Great Buddha Hall (*Daibutsuden*).

The *Kegon* school in Japan, more than being a sect, influenced many sects because of the richness of its thought content. In the *Shingon* sect organized by Kûkai, *Kegon* is placed on a higher level than *Tendai* and is recognized as the highest of the exoteric teachings (*Kenkyô*).

In the *Kegon* sect of the Kamakura period there was Myôe Shônin Kôben who excelled in scholarship and virtue (Rf. p. 11 ff.). Also Gyônen was famous for his writings, and moreover, he trained many disciples. Coming down to the Edo period, Hôtan sought to revive the *Kegon* school, and he produced many books.

The *Kegon* school has never been very large as a sect (Rf. p. 91). However, its influence which it exercised on the world through literature and art has been amazingly great, and it can be seen even in such a work as the *Tôkaidô Gojûsantsugi* (*The Fifty-Three Stages on the Tôkaidô Highway*) where the number is related to Zenzaidôji's travels in search of the Dharma in the *Nyûhokkaibon*. That the great Buddha of

Tôdaiji has supra-sectarian existence is clear when we observe the general interest that was mustered for the rebuilding of the hall of the Great Buddha in the Kamakura and Genroku periods. Later there will be an opportunity to clarify the true value of the *Kegon* sutra as a great treasure house of literature.

Hokke Faith

If one regards the *Kegon* sutra as an elegant literary production, the *Hokekyô* (*Saddharma-Pundarīka*) is a work of popular faith. The criticism to the effect that; "In order to know every distinctive feature of Mahayana Buddhism including both its weak points and strong points, there is no better way than to read the *Hokekyô*," (Winternitz) is very pertinent. We may regard the *Hokekyô* as having been composed about the second century.

The *Hokekyô* can be read today in the original Sanskrit, three types of Chinese translation, and in Tibetan translation, but, excluding some additions and deletions, there are not very striking differences in the texts. Even today the version translated by Kumārajīva in 406 is read in China and Japan. However, since there are also problems in the method of translation, and there are problematical points also in the lineage of his original text, it can by no means be recognized alone as the standard. The Sanskrit text is divided into twenty-seven chapters and the Chinese translation into twenty-eight. Most of the chapters are in two parts, both poetry and prose, and generally the composition of the poetic portions is older. All these chapters were probably not present together from the beginning, but new elements were gradually added to the perimeter of the core of the original sutra till it grew into the form as we presently see it. When we observe the Sanskrit text, the style is extremely rough and simple, and we can tell at a glance that it was written by the hand of people without very much education.

Following is the outline of the sutra: when Śākyamuni entered into *Samādhi* a mysterious phenomenon appeared. The disciples were astonished, and asked the reason for it. Then the Buddha answered that the Hinayana doctrine which he had taught up till that time was a temporary doctrine, and the true doctrine was the Mahayana teaching which he would relate thereafter. Men believe that Śākyamuni was born as a man and became Buddha after becoming enlightened in his place of practice near Gayā. But actually Buddha has been Buddha from the infinite past. He is unborn and undying. It is only to encourage sentient beings that he manifested himself in a form in which he died. This is the gist of *Hokekyô*.

So long as this *Hokekyô* is the most excellent sutra, a reward is promised to those who retain and hold it. Also sensuous joys of the ears, nose, tongue, body and mind are promised. Consequently, one should not fail to sacrifice something for the *Hokekyô*.

Besides the virtues which are promised to those who believe the *Hokekyô*, if the believers of the sutra are disparaged, reviled or slandered, the offenders will receive great punishment. However, those who keep this sutra must in their turn expect persecution.

Persecution is taught in the *Hokekyô* as prophecies entirely of future events. However, when we consider broadly other examples in religious literature, it is more reasonable to view them as describing the actual situation at the time of the composition of the sutra or as a possibility close at hand. In other words, at some time there existed a group that held the peculiar form of faith which corresponds to the original form of the *Hokekyô*. They gathered believers declaring that "Those who believed this doctrine, and cooperated in proclaiming it, would escape all suffering, be cured of disease, neither be burned by fire, nor drowned by water." In order to indicate the strength of this faith there were even some who poured oil on their own bodies and lit fire to it. When people who could not stand such persistency criticised them, they shouted, "Persecution!", and they stiffened their unity more and more. Then they themselves produced a text with the name *Hokekyô*. The people, generally, and particularly the orthodox Buddhist monks, were greatly disturbed, and they appealed to the king, ministers, general citizens and Buddhist monks. However, this fanatic group shouted: "Life is unimportant, the doctrine alone is important!" They continued to increase their activity. Thus the group developed, and by adding also new chapters and sections to the *Hokekyô* the form as it exists today was brought into being. This is the history of the composition of the *Hokekyô* which can be read from the text itself.

The *Hokekyô*, composed under such special conditions, some centuries afterward came to be recognized as a Mahayana sutra. That a sutra of a special group was adopted by the "church" in general is not rare in the history of religion. We can consider that its union with the Mahayana stream was achieved by the beginning of the Gupta dynasty.

However, a school centering on the *Hokekyô* was not formed at all in India. "Among all literary works this is something which absolutely rejects any thinking." (Watsuji Tetsurô). Therefore, Indian Buddhist philosophers did not regard the *Hokekyô* very highly. But in East Asia the situation became completely changed. There was probably no sutra as popular among the Chinese and Japanese as the *Hokekyô* which was translated at the beginning of the fifth century by Kumārajīva. The magical nature of the sutra, as we noted above, its fanaticism, and popular character captured the minds of men. Its spread extended in two directions, i.e., popular belief and exegetical study.

Suicidal acts called *shôshin* (burning the body) which imitated the tradition of the *Yakuôhonjibon* appear to have begun from the beginning of the period of North and South Dynasties in China, and there is an instance on record in 451. After that also *shôshin* continued to be performed, and I ching of T'ang also taught the harmful influence of "burning fingers, burning arms and burning the body." However, it was still performed even in the Sung period (there is a record from 983).

This custom was also transmitted to Japan, and a certain monk of Kôfukuji Temple who died in 973 is said to have peeled off the skin and burned his finger. A little before that there was a *Hokke* devotee who piled up firewood and, entering into it, cremated himself.

Together with the spread of the *Hokekyô* as the object of popular faith, there appeared after the North-South Dynasties those who wrote commentaries. Among the scholars of the *Kegon* sutra there were two or three who understood Sanskrit, but it is noteworthy that there were none at all among the interpreters of the *Hokekyô*. The trilogy of exegesis, interpretation and a guide-book for practice (*Makashikan*) by Chi I of the Sui period is the so-called *Tendaisandaibu* (Great Trilogy of *Tendai*) and forms the basis for the sect. However, it has no foundation in Indian tradition, and it is entirely a new Chinese interpretation. These commentators had the Chinese translation by Kumārajīva as their sole reference, but, to begin with, the authority of this Chinese translation is a problem.

For instance when we translate a passage of the *Hokekyô-hôbenbon* from the original Sanskrit text (the Tibetan translation also has the same text), it is as follows:

> Sāriputra, only a *Tathāgata* teaches to a *Tathāgata* all the *Dharma* which are known by a *Tathāgata*. Only a *Tathāgata* teaches all the *Dharma* completely. Only a *Tathāgata* knows all the *Dharma* completely. Only a *Tathāgata* sees what is before him and sees clearly (direct translation: it is not that he does not see clearly) concerning all the *Dharma*, that is to say, Which *Dharma*? What kind of *Dharma*? What manner of *Dharma*? *Dharma* possessing what type of traits? *Dharma* possessing what manner of self nature? In short, *Dharma* possessing which, what kind, what manner of traits and what manner of self nature?

According to the *Myôhôrengekyô Upadeśa* which Bodhiruci in the Latter Wei period translated (the different translation by Ratnamati of the Former Wei also has the same text):

> Sāriputra, only a Buddha teaches all *Dharma* to a Buddha. All the Buddhas and *Tathāgatas* can know the ultimate true traits (*Kugyô Jissô*) of those *Dharma*. Sāriputra, only Buddhas and *Tathāgatas* know all the *Dharma*. Sāriputra, only Buddhas and *Tathāgatas* can teach all *Dharma*, such as which *Dharma*? What manner of *Dharma*? How is it thus *Dharma*? *Dharma* (having) what traits? *Dharma* (having) what essence (nature)? What? What kind? What like? What traits? What essence? All *Dharma* such as these, a *Tathāgata* sees truly and he does not see unclearly.

When we compare this with the Sanskrit and Tibetan translation which we introduced above, it only differs on the points that the term "ultimate true traits" (*Kugyô Jissô*) is lacking and the order to "know" (*chi*) and "can teach" (*nôsetsu*) is changed in the Sanskrit and Tibetan versions. The rest is in complete agreement. Consequently, we can say that the Sanskrit text which was transmitted from India at the beginning of the sixth century does not differ greatly from the presently existing Sanskrit text. However, the passage according to the Chinese translation of Kumārajīva is completely different:

> Only a Buddha, therefore, can examine thoroughly (exhaustively) the true traits of all the *Dharma* for a Buddha. The various *Dharma* which are spoken of (are): Such is the trait; Such is the nature; Such is the essence (substance); Such is the power; Such is the production; Such is the cause; Such is the condition; Such is the fruit; Such is the recompense; Such is the ultimate substance and shadow. . . .

Kumārajīva's father was an Indian, but he was born of a Kuchan mother and his knowledge and materials concerning Buddhism derive primarily from Central Asia. Since his Chinese translation has as its main object to be easily understandable and easily read, his translation cannot be at all reliable in the strict sense.[1]

However, based on the above noted passages of Kumārajīva's translation, T'ien T'ai Ta shih Chi i began to speak of the *Jûnyoze* (Ten-thus-is) accepting the teaching of Nan yo Ta shih Hui ssu. He said:

> In (the phrase) *Jûnyoze* there are three ways of reading. If we read them *Zesônyo* (those traits are thus), *Zeshônyo* (the nature is thus) etc., it is the principle of *Kû* (Emptiness, *Sûnya*), and if we read them *Nyozesô* (Such is the trait), *Nyozeshô* (Such is the nature) etc., it is the principle of *Ke*, (Provisional, temporary). If we read them *Sônyoze* (the trait thus is), *Shônyoze* etc., it is true trait of the Middle Path, it is the principle of Middle (*Chû*).

Then he constructed *Tendai* doctrine based on the three truths of *Kû* (Emptiness), *Ke* (Provisional), and *Chû* (Middle). But, so long as the *Hokekyô* is a translation from the Sanskrit text, Chi I's interpretation does not hold good at all. Besides that, the theory of three truths as *Kû-Ke-*

---

[1] For instance, there are many points which have become problems also in his translations of the *Yuimagyô* (*Vimālakīrti nirdeśa*) and treatises related to the *Mādhyamika* school.

Chû used here also comes from a misunderstanding concerning the Indian Buddhist materials.[1] Accordingly, the entire *Tendai* doctrine was constructed by ignorance and misinterpretation.

The cause of this misinterpretation lies in the fact that from the beginning they have attempted to put the robes of doctrine on the *Hokekyô* which was originally popular and fanatic in nature. Actually, both in China and Japan *Tendai* doctrine had hardly any influence on thought in general. In the eighth century, Chan jan appeared, and wrote a commentary to the *Tendai sandaibu*. After this *Tendai* became compromising and composite, adopting elements of the *Kegon* school and others. Chan jan's disciple Tao sui taught Saichô the founder of our *Tendai* school in 806 at the Lung hsing ssu Temple in T'ai chou.

There was a stream of the *Hokke* faith apart from the doctrinal *Tendai* school. Besides those who cremated themselves, as we related before, *Hokke* believers called *jikyôja* (devotee of the *Hokekyô*) were in great number from about the Nara period in tales and literature. They transcended sect and doctrine and were people who earnestly believed in the spiritual experience of the *Hokekyô*. For instance, Kishin Shônin Jôyo, who was active about the beginning of the eleventh century, studied in the *Hossô* sect and was a person who tried to revive Kôyasan. He is outstanding as a *jikyôja*. Besides him, there were numberless, famous or nameless *jikyôja*, and they developed parallel with the followers of *Nembutsu* in the Middle Ages. It was the passionate Nichiren born in a

---

[1] With respect to the three truths of *Kû-Ke-Chû*, it is said that Hui wen gained insight by himself without (the assistance of) a teacher into the principle of *Isshin sankan* (Three aspects of one mind), according to a stanza of the *Mādhyamika śāstra*. This was transmitted to Chi I through Hui ssu. When we translate the stanza of the *Mādhyamika śāstra* from the Sanskrit text it states: "We call the (principle of) *Engi* (*Pratītyasamutpāda*) the 'nature of Emptiness' (*Kûshô*) and that is to be 'provisionally established' (*Kesetsu*-phenomenal) having foundation. It is the middle path itself." However, they are taught lining up three words having the same meaning in the background of Indian Buddhism, but when this fell into the hand of Chinese monks, we fear that they applied it to the organization of a totally unrelated theory.

fishing village by the eastern sea that balanced the general account of those *Hokke* devotees.

We have frequently touched on Nichiren above. When we summarize his standpoint there are two points:

1. The highest truth of Buddhism is the *Hokekyô* which is the true teaching of Śākyamuni.
2. Chi i and Saichô who interpreted this sutra were the greatest Buddhists, and Nichiren himself is the person most qualified to proclaim and put it into practice in the age of the decline of the *Dharma* (*Mappô*) in that he taught the prayer *Namu Myôhôrengekyô* which condenses the power of the sutra.

Nichiren believed the *Hokekyô* literally and, considering it all collectively as actual, he regarded himself as the central person. Then he corresponded with the officials of the Shôgunate and with the monks of the other sects, but no notice was taken of him. During that time social conditions and international conditions worsened. Nichiren, who thought of the *Dharma*, and thought of the country more and more, was carried away with impatience. His sense of opposition to his competitors increased. He gradually shifted adversaries. At first Hônen's *Nembutsu* was primary, and this remained his enemy until the last. Soon it turned out that *Zen* and *Nembutsu* were put side by side as his enemies. It was because of his individual hatred of the priest Ninshô that he attacked *Ritsu*. Ninshô was regarded as the instigator who had Nichiren banished to Sado. After he was banished to Sado, the order of his hatred became *Zen, Ritsu,* and *Nembutsu,* and soon it was altered to *Nembutsu, Shingon, Zen* and *Ritsu.* After he retired to Minobu, the order of his attack changed to *Shingon, Zen* and *Nembutsu.*

That he considered *Shingon* an immediate enemy was as a rival in prayers against the Mongols. He made, in contrast to that, both great teachers T'ien t'ai (Chi i) and Dengyô (Saichô) absolute objects of reverence. In his later years he came to say: "In the spread of the *Dharma,* Dengyô surpassed even T'ien t'ai (Chi i)." Finally, more than to establish a new sect Nichiren's true intention was to revive the *Tendai* school as pure *Hokke* faith.

As a theology Nichiren's teaching was quite simple, but his strong personality and simple popular nature captivated a portion of the people. The simple magical nature, sectarianism and combativeness of the *Hokekyô* manifested its original significance in Nichiren. In this sense, Nichiren and the modern quasi-religions rather than Chi i or Saichô, have grasped the original spirit of the *Hokekyô*.

Of sects which use the name of the founder in Japan there are not very many other than the *Nichiren* sect, but to the extent that they do individualism and exclusivism are all the more strong. Among the various Japanese sects there are only two closed religious communities, *Nichiren-shû* and *Jôdo Shinshû*. Consequently, both dispute with other sects and divisive activity within the sects is vehement. Divisions are frequently carried out by radicals. Besides the *Nichiren* sect, which has Mount Minobu as its central temple, there are several sects such as the *Nichiren Sôshû* and the *Hokkeshû* which have the headquarters of Nichiren's direct disciples as their central temples. In the Keichô era (circa 1596) one sect also of Nichiô, who advocated the uncompromising policy of "No give, no take" (*fujufuse*),[1] resisted repeated oppressions and became independent. Beginning with the *Hommon Butsuryûkô*, which commenced at the end of the Edo period, the *Reiyûkai* and the *Risshôkôseikai*, which began in the Taishô and Shôwa eras, belong to the so-called *Shinkôshû-kyô* (Newly arisen cults) which have as their object mass believers. The *Sôka Kyôiku Gakkai* which developed from a research organization of school teachers became the *Sôka Gakkai*, an auxiliary organization of the *Nichiren Sôshû*. At present those sects which are derived from the *Nichiren* school and officially registered as religious organizations, number as many as thirty. The peculiar traits of the *Nichiren* sect are its zeal and practicality. The adherents of the Nihonzan Myôhôji were loved by Gandhi because of their seriousness. It is also the people of the *Nichiren* sect who manifest the most zeal in opposition to tests of nuclear weapons. The figure of men emerging from exclusivism and sectarianism and striving for the sake of the peace of mankind is noble.

---

[1] Not receiving charity from the believers of non-*Nichiren* sects and not giving spiritual gifts to them.

Amida Faith

Amida faith along with *Hokke* faith was powerful in East Asia. It is known by the name *Jôdokyô* (Pure Land teaching).

In Mahayana Buddhism, it is thought that all the Buddhas exist simultaneously and to each Buddha belongs a respective Buddha land. *Sahā loka* (*Shaba Sekai*—our present finite world) in which we are now living is the Buddha land of Śākyamuni. There is Buddha everywhere, East, West, North and South, above and below, who has his land everywhere. Each Buddha-land has its peculiar traits, and is often considered the ideal land. We call each Buddha-land, the Pure Land (*Jôdo*). In contrast to the Pure Land, there also appeared a concept whereby our world is called the Defiled Land (*Edo*).

The Pure Lands are the same in number with the Buddhas; they are infinite. However, in China and Japan, the Pure Land of *Amida*, the world of Bliss (*Sukhāvatī*) became particularly famous.

Amida, in Chinese script is written 阿彌陀, but in Sanskrit, it is called *Amitābha* and translated as *Muryôkô-Butsu*. (the Buddha of Infinite Light). The name *Amitāyus,* Buddha of Infinite Life, (*Muryôju butsu*) is also frequently used. As in the case of all other Buddhas, when we look at it in its historical development, Buddhist concepts and the object of popular faith have probably blended. According to new research, a theory of Iranian origin for *Amida* is influential.

It is thought to be about the second century in Northwest India or in Central Asia that sutras related to *Amida* Buddha were composed and the concepts of the Buddha and the Pure Land got clearer definition. *Amida* Faith spread from the lands west of China, through China and also later to Tibet, but we cannot discover materials which positively demonstrate this for its spread in the Indian mainland. It does not appear either in the records of observations of Fa hsien, Hsuan tsang and I ching. Ts'u ming San t'sang Hui jih who traveled to India especially seeking *Amida* Faith also only said that he received a vision when he prayed to a *Kannon* (*Avalokiteśvara,* Bodhisattva of Mercy) image in the region of Gandhāra. In East Asia the *Muryôjukyô* (translated in 252 A.D.), the

Amidakyô (translated in 402 A.D.) and the *Kanmuryôjukô* (translated after 424 A.D.) are called the *Jôdo Sanbukyô* (*Tripartite Amitābha Sūtras*).

Chinese Pure Land teaching was formulated, based on two types of treatises which were translated into Chinese at about the same time as the above mentioned *Jôdo sambukyô*.

When Buddhism entered China, *Amida* Faith was soon introduced. In 402 Hui yuan established the *Pe lien she* on Lushan in Honan. Making his vow, he expected rebirth in the Western land of Bliss.

The origin of the Pure Land teaching as a sect in later times began with Tan luan at the end of the period of North-South dynasties. Seeking the methods of immortality in Taoism, he obtained the *Senkyô* (Secret book of Taoism). At Lohyang he met Bodhiruci and was given the *Kanmuryôjukyô*. After that he devoted himself to Pure Land faith and also exhorted others.

It was in the Sui period that Tao ch'o, who was born some twenty years after the death of Tan luan, read his epitaph and was deeply moved. He rejected scholarly study and was converted to the Pure Land faith. From this time the practice of reciting the *Nembutsu* and counting the number of times came to be widely diffused.

Among Tao cho's many disciples Shan tao completed the Chinese Pure Land teaching. He valued highly the practice of contemplation and his four volumed *Kanmuryôjukyôsho* (a commentary on *Kanmuryôju* sutra) became the foundation of Japanese Pure Land teaching.

The Buddha images which were known in the first period in our country were Śākyamuni and Maitreya (*Miroku*). Later *Yakushi*, *Kannon* and *Amida* became also popular. These reflect the fashions of the continent. It was after the middle of the Nara period that the worship of *Amida* became overwhelming.

The *Amida* faith of Japan from the beginning was developed also for the purpose of carrying out ceremonies for the dead and Buddhist memorial services. This primitive form of faith continued from Nara through the Heian period, and in the Kamakura era even after the Pure Land teaching was established as a pietism, it lived on till today as the practical function of the temples of each sect of Pure Land lineage.

From the beginning, *Nembutsu* elements were contained in Saichô's *Tendai* school. This was strengthened by his successors, and it was promoted for the spiritual enjoyment of the leisurely aristocrats represented by Fujiwara Michinaga.

On the one hand, it was the priest Kûya, a generation before Michinaga, who disseminated *Amida* faith for the common people (Rf. p. 34). Through the lifelong efforts of Kûya, the common people were given spiritual consolation and substantive relief, and they saw the practical side of Buddhism.

Among the scholarly priests of Mount Hiei, Eshin Sôzu Genshin authored the three volumed *Ôjôyôshû* (the Essentials of Salvation). In this work he compiled under various subjects important passages from sacred texts in Chinese translation relating to Hell, Pure Land, *Nembutsu* and Rebirth in Pure Land. It was not an original writing, but it came to be used widely as a textual basis for *Amida* faith. Aside from its contribution to the formation of the later Pure Land teaching, it also influenced literature and art.

Ryônin who was a priest performing miscellaneous services on Mount Hiei experienced a miracle of *Amida* Buddha, and he taught the *Nembutsu* for the sake of the common people. There were many followers among the people. His teaching is known as *Yûzûnembutsu* ("Circulation" of *Nembutsu*) from the point that the merit gained by an invocation of *Amida* was circulated and transferred to all sentient beings, so that the *Nembutsu* of one believer procured salvation for all others. It continues to today as an independent sect.

In the Kamakura period, Pure Land teaching was established for the first time as a powerful sect by Hônen (Rf. p. 31 ff.). The sole practice of *Nembutsu* (*Senju nembutsu*) which Hônen taught was the vocally recited *Nembutsu*. By just reciting the phrase *Namuamidabutsu* anyone could be born into *Amida*'s Pure Land of Bliss. This theory has as its textual basis the passage concerning the lowest beings of the lowest class (*gebon-geshô*) of the *Kanmuryôjukyô*. Because that time was the period of the civil wars and upheavals of the Taira and Minamoto clans, and dangers to life and property were frequent, the aristocrats and warriors

listened joyfully to this teaching of salvation. Later, Hônen's Pure Land
sect was divided into a few branches. The *Chinzei* branch which is
regarded as the orthodox line enjoyed the faith of the Emperor and the
nobles in Kyoto in the thirteenth century. In the fifteenth century the
Denzûin and Zôjôji temples were founded in Edo and flourished with
the support of the Tokugawa family. In the *Chinzei* branch Ryôyo
Shôgei, imitating the standards of *Mikkyô* etc., produced a rite called
the *Gojûsôden* and arranging its form as a sect, he laid the foundation of
today's Pure Land sect.

The most distinctive among Hônen's disciples was Shinran. He said
that he inherited Hônen's doctrine just as it was, but actually, he opened
an entirely new region. Shinran's standpoint was the eighteenth vow of
Amida in the *Muryôjukyô* and this he called "the vow of sincere faith."
Here *Jôdo Shinshû* which stands for absolute reliance upon Other Power
(*Tariki*) was born. Shinran himself rejected every contrivance and effort
for the sake of salvation, and attributed all virtue solely to the vow of
Amida Buddha.

In the words of the *Tannishô* also, Shinran's belief of absolute reliance
is manifested. Looking at it historically, the Pure Land faith, which at
first developed from *Amitābha*, (*Amida*) as the object of faith of a particular society, passed through a number of changes, and here in Shinran's thought overcame even the original object of rebirth in the Land
of Bliss to penetrate to a pure pietism.

As a result of Shinran's marriage, a Buddhist Order, in a form hitherto
unseen, developed. It consists of followers (*monto*) who had the descend-
ents of the founder Shinran in their center and the Honganji as the main
temple. If Shinran had not severed all relation with magic, probably his
official marriage would have been impossible in the formation of the
Order. By rejecting magic, a secular community was established, and he
could carry out evangelistic activity standing on the same level with the
believers. Further, because of its hereditary character, it could secure its
position as a feudal power or aristocracy. In this way the *Jôdo Shinshû*
sect, which is the greatest in Japanese Buddhism, was brought into being.

Ippen, who studied under a disciple of a disciple of Hônen, had a completely different method. Ippen, on the contrary, imitated the ancient Kûya Shônin, and he spread the *Nembutsu* among the common people. His footsteps spread widely through the whole country, and during sixteen years he recorded more than 250,000 believers. Almost all of them were ordinary common people. Abandoning difficult logic, he disseminated the Dancing *Nembutsu* (*Odori Nembutsu*) styled after Kûya. The greater part of the achievement in spreading the *Nembutsu* through the whole country can be said to be due to the succession of wandering holy priests who had Ippen as their founder. Today also, there is the *Jishû* sect which has the Shôjôkôji, or Yugyôji, as its main temple in Fujisawa in Kanagawa Prefecture, but the number of temples is less than 500, teachers 400 and followers 40,000. It is not very influential.

There is a minor, but noteworthy Pure Land sect of the same size which is called the *Tendai Shinzei* sect. This began on Mount Hiei in the fifteenth century when the priest Shinzei taught and practiced the unity of the recitation of *Nembutsu* and the *Endon* precepts. He went in the opposite direction of Hônen and Shinran. Shinzei's serious effort had influence on later generations.

Along with the fact that the *Nembutsu* became the possession of the common people, there appeared among the unlearned people, those also who opened a sphere of profound faith. These are called *myôkônin* (wonderously good men), and there are surprising things in their words and conduct.

While scholars of the Pure Land school are arguing why must the Pure Land of *Amida* be in the West, the unlearned believers quickly experience the truth that *Amida* Buddha does not exist apart from one's own mind (*Koshin Mida*, Rf. p. 137).

The influence which the spread of Pure Land doctrine had on our country was great. In this, the *Jôdo Shinshû* sect had influence on an unexpected area apart from Shinran's own intention. The denial of self power and the abandonment of the precepts permitted the promotion of a self-righteous and closed religious community. As we pointed out also earlier, in contrast to the fact that the men of the Sage path teaching (or self-enlightenment school, *Shôdômon*), which stands on the so-called "self power" (*Jiriki*), devoted themselves to social work, the *Shinshû* people, up till recent times, were disinterested in that area. Shinran's standpoint of *hisôhizoku* (neither priest nor layman) not only destroyed the discipline of the Order of those who renounced the world (monks), but it even completely trampled under foot the fundamental obligations of the lay believers. The first obligation of a Buddhist lay believer is offerings. The next is to observe the precepts for a layman. If one abolishes the offerings and precepts, it is clear in the history of the Order since India that the qualifications of a layman do not exist. Thus to call the teaching of Shinran, who abandoned even the qualifications of a lay believer, "Lay Buddhism" (*Zaike Bukkyô*) is entirely a misinterpretation. As Shinran himself said, he was neither a priest nor a layman.

Generally, the tendency also to a flight from reality in Pure Land doctrine is strong. It was Pure Land teaching also that promoted the attitude among the Japanese of avoiding facing a real problem face to face. Consequently, a great part of the responsibility also for cooperating with the feudal powers and obstructing the modernization of society lies here. Considering it from this point, we must say that the Pure Land teaching fulfilled a completely opposite function from the religious reformation in Europe. Such a biased view that has called this degenerated new religion "the essence of Japanese Buddhism" is prevalent even today among a segment of people. However, this assertion indicates that they do not know the true nature of Buddhism and its practical significance. The modernization of Pure Land teaching will be a problem in the future.

Conclusion

What has Buddhism taught the Japanese? On the positive side, it taught him to love mankind and mutually help each other, and that one should reverence all life. It indicated the ideal that at the same time that one perfects himself, he should make other men happy. Since Dôto first built the Uji Bridge, many Buddhists built roads, bridges and ponds and regulated rivers or planted trees in silence. Kûkai made a school for the common people (*Shugeishuchiin*), and he provided food for the teachers and the students. Ninshô built a hospital and helped leprosy patients. He also built a hospital for horses. Tetsugen gave food everyday to ten thousand famine-stricken people. There are also many other such examples. It was Buddhism also that taught reverence for life and had men give up the habit of eating meat. It was Buddhism also in an early age that caused the abolition of capital punishment. It was Buddhism also that taught the relation of man to man (even a chance meeting is due to the Karma in a previous life=even a chance acquaintance is pre-ordained), and pointed out the harmony of man and nature for us. In short, what is called humanism today we have primarily learned from Buddhism.

However, in sectarian Buddhism the formalized religious rituals and the mechanical way of thinking of the priests has made completely poverty stricken the religious activity of the Japanese. No one knows to what sect Ryôkan, who played handball with the children and went either to families who followed the *Nembutsu* or the *Hokekyô* and read the sutras, belonged. That is Buddhism. It may be sufficient if we construct a world such that it permits one to feel something warm in the hearts of people around him, and each is concerned with the other's welfare.

The main threads of Buddhism are the three studies of precepts, meditation and wisdom. With respect to social existence, moreover, before these the practice of offerings is required. We cannot call what departs from this main thread true Buddhism. It is natural that as times change and environment changes, also the form of Buddhism changes. However, only this fundamental principle is immovable. No matter how much one skillfully chops logic, if there is no seeking of *Bodhi*-mind (*jôgu-bodai*) above and the saving of beings below (*geke-shujô*), it is not Buddhism. What we call *jôgu-bodai* is to pursue the high ideal to the utmost for one's own sake and strive to realize a genuine Buddhist way of life. However, that must have the backing of the practice of *geke-shujô*, which means to strive to increase the happiness of all men. Apart from these, Buddhism is impossible.

Feudal Buddhism, which makes sectarian creeds central and adheres to formal religious ceremonies, conceals the true spirit of Buddhism. Even today, on the one hand, there are the already existing religious bodies which have grown weak with age and become powerless. On the other hand, the ignorant and violent newly arisen quasi-religions are clamoring. People who seek Buddhism from a liberal standpoint cannot find anything. A number of new Buddhist movements also arose during the Shôwa period (1926—), but in only the first two or three years were they pure. Soon they came into the hands of a few leaders who put on the airs of the head of a sect, and the upshot was that they declined to medieval "churches" no better than the already existing religious bodies. Organizations where only those who are partial gather and listen to lectures which imitate preaching are even more harmful for true Buddhist activity. If you ask why, it is because it gives rise to the hallucination that one participates in the *Dharma* unaccompanied by practical activities in benefiting others.

Today when the natural sciences have reached the stage where it is possible to destroy mankind at a blow, Buddhist humanism has become increasingly important. In order for Asian peoples to go hand in hand, it is also indispensable to have true Buddhism. If one considers that I have unhesitatingly offered criticisms in this book concerning Japanese Buddhism, past and present, it is only because I feel keenly the pressing need to cleanse thoroughly Buddhism which has become muddy and to restore again its original brilliance.

Selected *List* of Books on Japanese Buddhism

A. Bibliographies
Bando, Shôjun; Hanayama, Shôyû; Sato Ryôjun; Saeki Shinkô; Shima, Keiryû, *ed.*
   A Bibliography on Japanese Buddhism.
   Tokyo, The Cultural Interchange Institute for Buddhists, 1958.
Borton, Hugh; Elisséeff, Serge; Lockwood, William W.; Pelzel, John E., *ed.*
   A Selected List of Books and Articles on Japan in English, French and German.
      Cambridge, The Harvard-Yenching Institute, 1954 (revised and enlarged). (Buddhism: pp. 140–146).
K.B.S. *ed.*
   A Classified List of Works in Western Languages Relating to Japan. Part One.
      Tokyo, K.B.S., 1963. (Buddhism: pp. 125–131).
Kishimoto, Hideo, *ed.*
   K.B.S. Bibliography of Standard Reference Books for Japanese Studies with Descriptive Notes, Vol. IV: Religion.
      Tokyo, K.B.S., 1963. (Buddhism: pp. 51–106).

B. Dictionary
See K.B.S. Bibliography, Vol. IV: Religion.

C. Books on Japanese Buddhism
Anesaki, Masaharu
   History of Japanese Religion with Special Reference to the Social and Moral Life of the Nation.
      London, Kegan Paul, 1930.

Anesaki, Masaharu
  Nichiren, the Buddhist Prophet.
    Cambridge, Harvard University Press, 1916.
Ch'en, Kenneth K.S.
  Buddhism, The Light of Asia.
    New York, Barron's Educational Series, Inc., 1968.
Coates, Harper Havelock & Ishizuka, Ryugaku, *tr.*
  Hônen, the Buddhist Saint. His Life and Teachings.
    Kyoto, Chion'in, 1925.
Eliot, Sir Charles
  Japanese Buddhism.
    London, Arnold, 1935.
Florenz, Karl
  Der japanische Buddhismus (Chantepie de la Saussaye; *Lehrbuch der Religionsgeschichte.* Tübingen, 1927, pp. 348–422).
Hashikawa, Tadashi
  Gaisetsu Nihon Bukkyôshi (An Outline History of Japanese Buddhism).
    Tokyo, Heirakuji Shoten, 1929 (1st ed.), 1961.
Hashikawa, Tadashi
  Sôgô Nihon Bukkyôshi (A Comprehensive History of Japanese Buddhism).
    Tokyo, Meguro Shoten, 1932.
Kohler, Werner
  Die Lotus-Lehre und die modernen Religionen in Japan.
    Zürich, Atlantis Verlag, 1962.
Murakami, Senshô
  Nihon Bukkyôshi Kô (An Outline of the History of Japanese Buddhism), 2 vols.
    Tokyo, Kinkôdô, 1898–9 (1st ed.); Tokyo, Sôgensha, 1925 (2nd ed.).
Reischauer, A. K.
  Studies in Japanese Buddhism.
    New York, Macmillan, 1925.
Rosenberg, Otto
  Die Probleme der buddhistischen Philosophie, Materialien zur Kunde des Buddhismus, tr. from the Russian by E. Rosenberg.
    Heidelberg, Harrassowitz, 1924.
Sansom, George Bailey
  Japan, A Short Cultural History (The Cresset Historical Series).
    London, Cresset, 1931; New York, Appleton Century, 1943, 1952.

Takakusu, Junjiro
  The Essentials of Buddhist Philosophy, ed. by W. T. Chan & C. A. Moore.
    Honolulu, University of Hawaii, 1947.
Shimaji, Daitô
  Nihon Bukkyô Kyôgakushi (History of Buddhist Doctrine in Japan).
    Tokyo, Meiji Shoin, 1933.
Tsuji, Zennosuke
  Nihon Bukkyôshi (History of Japanese Buddhism), 10 vols.
    Tokyo, Iwanami Shoten, 1944–55; 1960–61 (2nd print).
Uehara, Senroku; Kamei, Katsuichiro; Furuta, Shokin; Nakamura,
Hajime, *ed.*
  Gendai Bukkyô Kôza (Lecture Series on Contemporary Buddhism),
  5 vols.
    Tokyo, Kadokawa, 1955.
Ui, Hakuju
  Nihon Bukkyô Gaishi (A Short History of Japanese Buddhism)
    Tokyo, Iwanami Shoten, 1951.
Ui, Hakuji
  Bukkyô Hanron (A Survey of Buddhism).
    Tokyo, Iwanami Shoten, 1962.

Table of Important Dates on Japanese Buddhism

A.D.

538 The official introduction of Buddhism from Paekche by the sending of Buddha images, etc. (one theory holds 552).

590 Zenshinni and other nuns return (they went to Paekche in 588).

593   Shôtoku Taishi, Regent (—621).

602 Paekche monk Kanroku comes.

624 Monk system determined.

645   Taika Reform.

646 Dôtô builds Uji Bridge first time.

657 Beginning of *Urabon-e*.

672   Civil War of *Jinshin*.

673 Copying of entire Buddhist Canon.

699 En'no Gyôja banished to Izu.

700 Death of Dôshô; beginning of practice of cremation in Japan.

710   Nara made the capital.

718 Dôji returns (went to T'ang China in 701).

729 Chikô and Raikô study *Sanron* under Chizô about this time.

736 Indian monk Bodhisena, Vietnam monk Buttetsu from Rinyû (or Campa) and T'ang monk Tao hsüan come to Japan.

740 Rôben attends the Silla monk Shinjo's lecture on *Kegon* sutra.

741 Gyôhyô and others take orders under Tao hsüan.

745 Gyôgi becomes chief abbot.

752 Dedication of Great Buddha of Tôdaiji Temple.

754 T'ang monks Chien chen (Ganjin), Fa chin (Hôshin) and others come to Japan.

755 Tôdaiji Ordination Hall built.

785 Saichô builds a hermitage on Mount Hiei.

794   Heian (present Kyoto) becomes the capital.

805 Saichô returns (went to T'ang the year before); begins the *Tendai* school.

806 Kûkai returns (804 went to T'ang); begins *Shingon* school.

818 Genpin dies.

822 Saichô dies. Permission granted for establishing Ordination Platform on Mount Hiei.

835 Kûkai dies.

847 En'nin returns (838 went to T'ang).

858 Enchin returns (853 went to T'ang)   Beginning of Fujiwara Regency.

865 Shinnyo Hôshinnô dies.

884 Activity of An'nen at this time.

894   Cessation of dispatching envoys to T'ang China.

938 Kûya teaches *Nembutsu*.

985 Genshin writes *Ôjôyôshû*.

987 Chônen returns (went to Sung in 982).

1003 Jakushô enters Sung.

1028 Jôyo strives to revive Mount Kôya.

1086   Beginning of *Insei* (cloister government).

1124 Ryônin teaches *Nembutsu*; beginning of *Yûzûnembutsu* school.

1136 Kakuban moves from Mount Kôya to Negorosan.

1150	Hônen studies *Nembutsu* under Eikû.
1156	*Hôgen* civil war.
1159	*Heiji* civil war.
1168	Chôgen returns (year before he went to Sung). Eisai goes and returns from Sung in this year.
1175	Hônen teaches the *Senjunembutsu*; beginning the *Jôdo* school.
1191	Eisai returns (went again to Sung in 1187); beginning of the *Rinzai* school.
1192	Beginning of the Kamakura Shogunate.
1211	Shunjô returns (went to Sung in 1199).
1212	Kôben writes *Zaijarin*.
1224	Shinran begins to write *Kyôgyôshinshô* about this time; beginning of the *Jôdo Shinshû* school. Myôhen dies.
1227	Dôgen returns (1223 went to Sung); begins *Sôtô Zen* school.
1246	Sung monk Lan Ch'i Tao lung (Rankei Dôryû) comes to Japan.
1253	Nichiren active in Kamakura; begins *Nichiren* school.
1260	Sung monk Wu an Pu ning (Gottan Funei) comes to Japan.
1276	Ippen teaches Dancing *Nembutsu*; begins *Jishû* school.
1280	Yuan monk We hsuen Tsu yuan (Mugaku Sogen) comes to Japan.
1281	Mongol invasion, *Kôan* War.
1286	Eizon completes Uji Bridge.
1290	Nichikô founds Daisekiji Temple.
1294	Ninshô restores the Hiden'in and Keiden'in of Shiten'nôji Temple. Nichizô active in Kyoto.
1297	Yuan monk I shan I ning (Issan Ichinei) comes to Japan.
1298	Nichimoku becomes abbot of Daisekiji Temple.

1321	Gyônen dies.	
1322	Eizan (Keizan) Shôkin founds Sôjiji Temple.	
1324	The author of *Tsurezuregusa*, Kenkô, retires to his hermitage.	
1334		Restoration of Kemmu.
1336		Beginning of Muromachi Shogunate.
1339	Musô Soseki founds the Tenryûji Temple.	
1342	Daikaku becomes abbot of Myôkenji Temple.	
1365	Gasan Shôseki dies.	
1392		Unification of North and South courts.
1394	Myôchô becomes the Densu (the warden) of Tôfukuji Temple.	
1415	Ryôyo Shôgei founds the Denzûin.	
1467		*Ônin* civil war.
1469	Priest painter, Sesshû, returns (previous year he went to Sung).	
1483	Shinzei enters *Nembutsu*; begins *Tendai Shinzei* school.	
1487	Revolt of the Ikkô followers (*Jôdo Shinshû*) in Kaga.	
1536	*Tem'mon Hokke* revolt.	
1549		Xavier transmits Catholicism.
1571	Nobunaga burns Hieizan.	
1580	Ken'nyo of the Honganji withdraws from Ishiyama castle in Osaka.	
1584	Zon'nô becomes abbot of Zôjôji Temple.	
1585	Hideyoshi burns Negorosan and forces Mount Kôya to surrender.	Hideyoshi becomes regent.
1602	Myônin and others plan revival of *Ritsu* school.	
1603		Beginning of Edo Shôgunate.

1612   Tenkai meets Ieyasu for the first time.

1619   Sûden becomes Sôrokushi (in charge of recording Buddhist monks).

1623   Nichiô advocates *Fujufuse* (no give, no take).

1635   First time for establishing Jishabugyô (a commissioner of temples and shrines in Edo government).

1638   Takuan founds Tôkaiji Temple.

1639   Beginning of a National Isolation Policy.

1651   Ming monk Tao che Ch'ao yuan (Dôsha Chôgen) comes to Japan (returns to China in 1658).

1654   Ming monk Yin yuan Lung ch'i (Ingen Ryûki) comes to Japan; beginning of *Ôbaku Zen* school.

1655   Ming monk Mu an Hsing tao (Mokuan Shôtô) comes to Japan.

1661   Ming monk Kao chuan Hsin tun (Kôsen Shôtô) comes.

1676   Shidô Bunan (Munan) dies.

1677   Keichû studies *Siddham* under Jôgon.

1678   Myôryû chased from Mount Hiei.

1681   Tetsugen completes publication of *Issai kyô* (entire Buddhist canon).

1683   Tôsui Unkei dies.

1688   Genroku period (—1703).

1693   Reikû makes the Anrakuin into a Ritsuin (*Vinaya* temple).

1699   Manzan Dôhaku plans to revive *Sôtô* school.

1708   Hakuin studies under Dôkyô Etan.

1736   Jakugon studies *Siddham* under Donjaku.

1744   Onkô advocates orthodox precepts.

1804   Ryôkan builds Gogôan retreat.

1867   Restoration of Imperial government.

1873   Shimaji Mokurai returns from travels
       in Europe and India (he left Japan the
       previous year).

1924   Gonda Raifu travels to China and be-
       stows the consecration of transmitting
       the esoteric *Dharma*.

1956   Participation of many Japanese in the
       celebration of the 2500 year anniversary
       of Buddha's *Jayanti* in India.

Index Personarum
relating Japanese Buddhism

W

Wu hsueh Tsu yuan 無学祖元, *see* Mugaku Sogen

Y

Yin yuan Lung ch'i 隠元隆琦, *see* Ingen Ryûki
Yôsai 栄西, *see* Eisai

Z

Bibliographical Works

Adams, Charles J. (ed.): *A Reader's Guide to the Great Religions*. New York, 1965.

Bandô Shôjun & others (ed.): *A Bibliography on Japanese Buddhism*. Tokyo, CIIB Press, 1958.

Ebisawa, Arimichi: *Christianity in Japan. A Bibliography of Japanese and Chinese Sources. Part I, 1543–1858*. Tokyo, Kirisutokyô Shigakkai, 1930.

Earhart, H. Byron: *The New Religions of Japan. A Bibliography of Western-Language Materials*. Tokyo, Sophia University (*Monumenta Nipponica*), 1970.

Hanayama, Shinshô: *Bibliography on Buddhism*. Tokyo, Hokuseidô, 1961.

Holzman, Donald & others (ed.): *Japanese Religion and Philosophy: A Guide to Japanese Reference and Research Materials*. Michigan, University of Michigan, 1959.

K.B.S. (ed.): *K.B.S. Bibliography of Standard Reference Books for Japanese Studies with Descriptive Notes. Vol. IV: Religion*. Tokyo, University of Tokyo Press, 1963.

———: *K.B.S. Bibliography of Standard Reference Books for Japanese Studies with Descriptive Notes. Vol. V-A: History of Thought (Parts I & II)*. Tokyo, University of Tokyo Press, 1965.

Sasaki, Ruth Fuller: "A Bibliography of Transactions of Zen (Ch'an) Works," *Philosophy East and West*, X (Nos. 3–4, October, 1960-January, 1961), 149–66.

Shulman, Frank J. (comp. & ed.): *Japan and Korea, An Annotated Bibliography of Doctoral Dissertations in Western Languages, 1877–1969*.

Japanese Religion and Philosophy, pp. 221–232. Chicago, American Library Association, 1970.

Dictionaries

Humphreys, Christmas: *A Popular Dictionary of Buddhism,* New York Citadel, 1963.

Japanese-English Buddhist Dictionary. Tokyo, Daitô Shuppansha, 1965.

Shintô Committee for the IXth International Congress for the History of Religions: *Basic Terms of Shintô.* Tokyo, Institute for Japanese Culture and Classics, 1958.

General Works

Anesaki, Masaharu: *History of Japanese Religion; with Special Reference to the Social and Moral Life of the Nation.* Tokyo & Rutland, Vt., Charles E. Tuttle, 1963.

Basabe, Fernando M.: *Religious Attitudes of Japanese Men; a Sociological Survey.* Tokyo, Sophia University (*Monumenta Nipponica* Monograph), 1968.

Beck, L. Adams: *The Story of Oriental Philosophy.* New York, New Home Library 1931.

Bellah, R. N.: *Tokugawa Religion.* Glencoe, Ill., Free Press, 1957.

Benedict, Ruth: *The Chrysanthemum and the Sword: Patterns of Japanese Culture.* Boston, Houghton Mifflin, 1946.

Bunce, William K. (ed.): *Religions in Japan; Buddhism, Shintô, Christianity.* Tokyo & Rutland, Vt., Charles E. Tuttle, 1955.

Callaway, Tucker N.: *Japanese Buddhism and Christianity.* Tokyo, Shinkyô Shuppansha, 1957.

Earhart, H. Byron: *Japanese Religion; Unity and Diversity.* Belmont, Dickenson Publishing Co., 1969.

Embree, John F.: "Some Social Functions of Religion in Rural Japan," *American Journal of Sociology,* No. 47 (1941), pp. 284–89.

Griffis, William E.: *The Religions of Japan; From the Dawn of History to the Era of Meiji.* New York, Charles Scribner, 1901.

Hammer, Raymond: *Japan's Religious Ferment*. New York, Oxford University Press, 1962.

Harada, Tasuku: *The Faith of Japan*. New York, Macmillan, 1924.

Hearn, Lafcadio: *Japan's Religions: Shinto and Buddhism*. Ed. by Katô Kazumitsu. University Books, Inc., 1966.

Heaslett, Samuel: *The Mind of Japan and the Religions of the Japanese*. (Religions of the East Series, No. 1.), London, The Churches' Committee for Work among Men in H. M. Forces, 1947.

Institute for Research in Religious Problems: *Religions in Japan at Present*. Tokyo, IRRP, 1958.

International Institute for the Study of Religions: *Religion and Modern Life* (Bulletin No. 5, Part II). Tokyo, IISR, 1958.

————: *Religion and State in Japan* (Bulletin No. 7). Tokyo, IISR, 1959.

Kishimoto, Hideo (ed.): *Japanese Religion in the Meiji Era*. Trans. by J. F. Howes. Tokyo, Tôyôbunko, 1970.

Kitagawa, Joseph M.: *Religion in Japanese History*. New York, Columbia University Press, 1966.

Knox, George W.: *The Development of Religion in Japan*. New York, Putnam, 1907.

Mombushô: *Religions in Japan*, Tokyo, Religious Affairs Section, Research Bureau, Ministry of Education, 1959.

Moor, George F.: *History of Religions*. Vol. 1. New York, Scribner, 1913–26.

Morioka, Kiyomi and William H. Newell (ed.): *The Sociology of Japanese Religion*. Leiden, Brill (*International Studies in Sociology and Social Anthropology*, Vol. 6), 1968.

Nihon Shûkyô Gakkai (The Japanese Association for Religious Studies): *Religion East and West; No. 3. Special Edition of Journal of Religious Studies*. Tokyo, NSG., 1966. (Current Tends of Shintô, Buddhist and Christian Studies in Japan).

Piovesana, Gino K.: *Recent Japanese Philosophical Thought 1862–1962. A Survey*. Tokyo, Enderle, 1963.

Reischauer, August K.: *The Nature and Truth of the Great Religions, to-*

ward a Philosophy of Religion. Tokyo & Rutland, Vt., Charles E. Tuttle, 1966.

Underwood, Horace G.: *The Religions of Eastern Asia.* New York, Macmillan, 1910.

Shinto

Akiyama, Aisaburô: *Shintô and its Architecture.* Kyoto, Kinki Kantô Kyôkai, 1936.

Anesaki, Masaharu: *Japanese Mythology.* (Vol. VIII of *The Mythology of All Races,* ed. C. J. A. MacCulloch) Boston, Marshall Jones, 1928.

Anzu, Motohiko: *Fundamental Elements of Shintô Rituals.* Tokyo, Nippon Bunka Chûô Renmei, 1941.

Ariga, Tetsutarô: "Contemporary Apologetics of Shintô," Missionary Research Library, *Occasional Bulletin,* Vol. V (No. 5, April, 1954).

Aston, William G.: *Shintô, The Way of the Gods.* London, Longmans, Green, 1905.

———: *Shintô; the Ancient Religion of Japan.* London Constable, 1921.

Ballou, Robert O.: *Shintô, the Unconquered Enemy.* New York, Viking Press, 1945.

Creemers, Wilhelmus H. M.: *Shrine Shintô fter World War II.* Leiden Brill, 1968.

Hepner, Charles W.: *The Kurozumi Sect of Shintô.* Tokyo, Meiji Japan Society, 1935.

Hibino, Yutaka: *Nippon Shindô Ron or the National Ideals of the Japanese People.* Tr. A. P. McKenzie. Cambridge, Cambridge University Press, 1928.

Hirai, Naofusa: "The Concept of Man in Shintô." Unpublished Master's dissertation. Chicago, University of Chicago, 1954.

———: "Fundamental Problems of Present Shintô," *Proceedings of the IXth International Congress for the History of Religions* (Tokyo, 1960), pp. 303–6.

Holtom, Daniel C.: *Modern Japan and Shintô Nationalism; A Study of Present-day Trends in Japanese Religions.* Chicago, University of Chicago Press, 1947.

———: *The National Faith of Japan. A Study in Modern Shintô*. London, Paul, Trench, Trubner, 1938.

———: "Some Notes on Japanese Tree Worship," *TASJ*, Second Series, VIII (December, 1931), 1–19.

———: "The Meaning of Kami," *Monumenta Nipponica* III, No. 1 (1940), 1–27; III, No. 2, 32–53; IV, No. 2 (1941), 25–68.

———: "Shin-tô in the Postwar World," *Far Eastern Survey*, No. 14 (February 14, 1945), pp. 29–33.

———: "Shintoism," in *The Great Religions of the Modern World*, ed. Edward J. Jurii (Princeton, 1946), pp. 141–77.

Hozumi, Nobushige: *Ancestor Worship and Japanese Law*. Tokyo, Maruya, 1901.

Jinja-honchô (ed.): *An Outline of Shintô Teaching*. Compiled by Shintô Committee for the IXth International Congress for the History of Religion. Tokyo, Jinja-honchô, 1958.

———: *Basic Teaching of Shintô*. Compiled by Shintô Committee for the IXth International Congress for the History of Religion. Tokyo, Jinja-honchô, 1958.

———: *Shintô Shrines and Festivals*. Compiled by Shintô Committee for the IXth International Congress for the History of Religion. Tokyo, Jinja-honchô, 1958.

Katô, Genchi: *A Study of Shintô, the Religion of the Japanese Nation*. Tokyo, Meiji Japan Society, 1926.

———: *What is Shintô?* Tokyo, Board of Tourist Industry, 1935.

Mason, John Warren Teets.: *The Meaning of Shintô; the Primaeval Foundation of Creative Spirit in Modern Japan*. New York, E. P. Dutton, 1935.

———: *The Spirit of Shintô Mythology*. Tokyo, Fuzambô, 1939.

———: *The Meaning of Shintô; the Primaeval Foundation of Creative Spirit in Modern Japan*. Port Washington, N.Y., Kennikat Pr., 1967.

Moore, Charles A. (ed.): *The Japanese Mind; Essentials of Japanese Philosophy and Culture*. Honolulu, University of Hawaii Press, 1967.

Muraoka, Tsunetsugu: *Studies in Shintô Thought*. Tr. by Delmer M. Brown and James T. Araki. Tokyo, Mombushô, 1964.

Omi, T.: *Mythology of Japan*. Tokyo, Suzambô, 1915.

Ono, Sokyo: *The Kami Way; An Introduction to Shrine Shintô*. Tokyo & Rutland, Vt., Charles E. Tuttle, 1960.

Philippi, Donald L.: *Norito; A New Translation of the Ancient Japanese Ritual Prayers*. Tokyo, Kokugakuin University, 1959.

Pigott, Juliet: *Japanese Mythology*. Felpham, Middlesex Paul Hamlyn, 1969.

Ponsonby-Fane, R. A. B.: *The Vicissitudes of Shintô*. Kyoto, Ponsonby Memorial Society, 1963.

———: *Visiting Famous Shrines in Japan*. Kyoto, Ponsonby Memorial Society, 1963.

Ross, Floyd H.: *Shintô, the Way of Japan*. Boston, Beacon Press, 1965.

Satow, E. M.: "The Shinto Shrines of Ise," *TASJ*, III, Part I (Supplement, 1875; rev., 1882), 1–87.

Schneider, Delwin B.: *Konkôkyô: A Japanese Religion*. Tokyo, International Institute for the Study of Religions, 1962.

Schurhammer, George: *Shin-Tô: the Way of the Gods in Japan*. Leipzig, Kurt Schroder, 1923.

Schwartz, W. L.: "The Great Shrine of Idzumo, "*TASJ,* XLI (Part 4, October, 1913), 493–681.

Shintô Shôgakukai: *Sectarian Shintô*. (The Way of the Gods). Tokyo, Japan Times & Mail, 1937.

Staelen, H. Van: *The Religion of Divine Wisdom*. Tokyo, Veritas Shoin, 1957.

Tenshô-Kotai-Jingû-kyô: *The Prophets of Tabuse*. Tabuse, 1954.

———: *Guidance to God's Kingdom*. Tabuse, 1956.

Toda, Yoshio: "Traditional Tendency of Shintoism and Its New Theoretical Developments," in *Religious Studies in Japan,* ed. Japanese Association for Religious Studies (Tokyo, 1959), pp. 229–32.

Underwood, A. C.: *Shintoism; the Indigenous Religion of Japan*. London, Epworth Press, 1934.

Buddhism

Armstrong, R. C.: *Buddhism and Buddhists in Japan*. New York, Macmillan, 1927.

Bloom, Alfred: *Shinran's Gospel of Pure Grace.* University of Arizona Press, 1965.

Blyth, R. H.: *Zen and Zen Classics.* 4 vols. Tokyo, Hokuseidô, 1960–70.

Briggs, William A.: *Anthology of Zen.* Grove, 1961.

Bukkyô Dendô Kyôkai: *The Teaching of Buddha.* Tokyo, BDK, 1970.

Coates, Harper H., and Ishizuka, Ryûgaku: *Hônen the Buddhist Saint,* Kyoto, Chion-in, 1925.

Conze, Edward: *Buddhism; its Essence and Development.* New York, Farber & Farber, 1951.

De Bary, William Theodore (ed.): *The Buddhist Tradition in India, China and Japan.* New York, Modern Library, 1969.

De Visser, Marius W.: *Ancient Buddhism in Japan; Sûtras and Ceremonies in Use in the Seventh and Eighth Centuries A.D. and their History in Later Times.* Leiden, E. J. Brill, 1928–35.

Dumoulin, Heinrich: *A History of Zen Buddhism.* Tr. Paul Peachery. New York, Farber & Farber, 1963.

Eliot, Sir Charles N. E.: *Japanese Buddhism.* London, Edward Arnold, 1935.

Elisséeff, Serge, and Matsushita, Takaaki: *Japan's Ancient Buddhist Paintings.* Greenwich, Conn. New York Graphic Society, 1959.

Enomiya-Lassale, Hugo M.: *Zen-Way to Enlightenment.* New York, Taplinger, 1968.

Fujikawa, Asako: *Ogozen; Daughter of Shinran.* Tokyo, Hokuseidô, 1964.

Fujiwara, Ryôsetsu (tr. & annot.): *The Tanni Shô: Notes Lamenting Differences.* Kyoto, 1962.

Haguri, Gyodo: *The Awareness of Self; a Guide to the Understanding of Shin Buddhism.* Kyoto, private, 1967.

Hanayama, Shinshô: *A History of Japanese Buddhism.* Tr. & ed. Koshô Yamamoto. Tokyo, CIIB Press, 1960.

———: *The Way of Deliverance.* Tr. Hideo Suzuki, Eiichi Noda, and James K. Sasaki. London, Victor Gollancz, 1955.

Herrigel, Eugen: *Zen in the Art of Archery.* London, Routledge & Kegan Paul, 1956.

Hompa Honganji Mission of Hawaii: *The Shinshu Seiten; or the Holy*

Scripture of Shinshu. Honolulu, HHMH, 1961.

Hori, Ichirô: "Buddhism in the Life of Japanese People," in *Japan and Buddhism,* ed. The Association of the Buddha Jayanti (Tokyo, 1959).

———: "Self-Mummified Buddhas in Japan," *History of Religions,* I (No. 2, Winter, 1962), 222–42.

Humphreys, Christmas: *Zen Buddhism.* London, Unwin Books, 1961.

Kamstra, J. H.: *Encounter or Syncretism; the Initial Growth of Japanese Buddhism.* Leiden, E. J. Brill, 1967.

Kapleau, Philip (comp. & ed.): *The Three Pillars of Zen; Teaching, Practice, and Enlightenment.* Tokyo, John Weatherhill, 1965.

Lillie, Arthur: *Buddha and Buddhism.* Edinburgh, Clark, 1900.

Lloyd, Arthur: *Buddhist Meditations from the Japanese;* with an introductory chapter on modern Japanese Buddhism. Tokyo, Rikkyô Gakuin, 1905.

Lloyd, Arthur: *The Creed of Half Japan.* (Historical sketches of Japanese Buddhism.) London, John Murray, 1911.

Leggett, Trevor (comp. & tr.): *A First Zen Reader.* Tokyo & Rutland, Vt., Charles E. Tuttle, 1963.

Matsunaga, Alicia: *The Buddhist Philosophy of Assimilation; the Historical Development of the Honji-suijaku Theory.* Tokyo, Sophia University, 1969.

Reischauer, A. K.: *Studies in Japanese Buddhism.* New York, Macmillan, 1925.

Reischauer, Edwin O.: *Ennin's Diary; the Record of a Pilgrimage to China in Search of the Law.* New York, Ronald Press, 1955.

———: *Ennin's Travels in T'ang China.* New York, Ronald Press, 1955.

Reps, Paul: *Zen Flesh, Zen Bones.* Tokyo & Rutland, Vt., Charles E. Tuttle, 1958.

Rhys-Davids, T. W.: *Buddhism; a Study of the Buddhist Norm.* London, Williams & Norgate, n.d.

———: *Buddhism; its History and Literature.* New York, Putnam, 1901.

———: *Early Buddhism.* London, Constable, 1910.

Richard, Timothy: *The New Testament of Higher Buddhism.* Edinburgh, Clark, 1910.

Ross, Nancy W. (comp. & ed.): *The World of Zen; and East-West Anthology*. London, Collins, 1962.

Sandilyayana Rastrapala: *A Short History of Early Japanese Buddhism*. Tokyo, International Buddhist Society, 1940.

Sasaki, Gesshô: *A Study of Shin Buddhism*. Kyoto, Eastern Buddhist Society, 1925.

Saunders, E. Dale: *Buddhism in Japan; with an Outline of its Origins in India*. Philadelphia, University of Pennsylvania, 1964.

———: *Mudrâ; a Study of Symbolic Gestures in Japanese Buddhist Sculpture*. New York, Pantheon Books, 1960.

Shacklock, Floyd: *Some Aspects of the Influence of Western Philosophy upon Japanese Buddhism*. Tokyo, Kyôbunkwan, 1939.

Shinran: *Tannishô; a Tract Deploring Heresies of Faith*. Tokyo, Higashi Honganji, 1962.

Steinilber-Oberlin, E.: *The Buddhist Sects of Japan; their History, Philosophical Doctrines and Sanctuaries*. London, George Allen & Unwin, 1938.

Suzuki, Daisetsu T.: *The Essentials of Zen Buddhism; An Anthology of the Writings of Daisetsu T. Suzuki*. London, New York, Rider, 1963.

———: *Shin Buddhism*. New York, Harper & Row, 1970.

———: *Zen and Japanese Buddhism*. Tokyo, Japan Tourist Bureau, 1961.

Tachibana, S.: *The Ethics of Buddhism*. London, Oxford University Press, 1926.

Takagi, Shunshi: *Biographical Sketches of the East-West Buddhologists*. Tokyo, Karinbunko, 1970.

Takeuchi, Yoshinori: "Shinran's Religious Philosophy." (Mimeographed lecture notes, Columbia University, 1962.)

Tannishô Kenkyûkai (ed.): *Perfect Freedom in Buddhism; an Exposition of the Words of Shinran, Founder of the Shin Sect*. 1968.

Thomas, Edward J.: *The History of Buddhist Thought*. London, Kegan Paul, Trench, Trubner, 1927.

Ueda, Daisuke: *Zen and Science*. Tokyo, Risôsha, 1963.

Ui, Hakuju: "A Study of Japanese Tendai Buddhism," *Philosophical Studies of Japan*, Vol. I, ed. Japanese National Commission for Unesco (Tokyo, 1959), pp. 33–74.

Waley, Arthur: *Zen Buddhism and its Relation to Art.* London, Luzac, 1959.

Watanabe, Shôkô: *Japanese Buddhism; a Critical Appraisal.* Tokyo, Kokusai Bunka Shinkokai, 1964, 1970.

Wienpahl, Paul: *The Matter of Zen; a Brief Account of Zazen.* New York University, 1964.

Yamakami, Sôgen: *System of Buddhist Thought.* Calcutta, 1912.

Yamamoto, Koshô: *An Introduction to Shin Buddhism.* Ube, Karinbunko, 1963.

———: *The Other-power; the Final Answer Arrived at in Shin Buddhism.* Ube, Karinbunko, 1965.

———: *The Private Letters of Shinran Shônin.* Tokyo, 1956.

Confucianism

Armstrong, Robert C.: *Light from the East; Studies in Japanese Confucianism.* Toronto, University of Toronto, 1914.

Hall, John Whitney: "The Confucian Teacher in Tokugawa Japan," *Confucianism in Action,* ed. David S. Nivison and Arthur F. Wright (Stanford, 1959), pp. 268–301.

Shively, Donald H.: "Motoda Eifu: Confucian Lecturer to the Meiji Emperor," *Confucianism in Action,* ed. David S. Nivison and Arthur F. Wright (Stanford, 1959), pp. 302–33.

Smith, Warren W., Jr.: *Confucianism in Modern Japan: A Study of Conservatism in Japanese Intellectual History.* Tokyo, Hokuseidô, 1959.

Christianity

Anesaki, Masaharu: *A Concordance to the History of Kirishitan Missions.* (Catholic Missions in Japan in the 16th and 17th Centuries.) Tokyo, Imperial Academy, 1930.

———: *Writing on Martyrdom in Kirishitan Literature.* Tokyo, Asiatic Society of Japan, 1931.

Best, Earnest E.: *Christian Faith and Cultural Crisis. The Japanese Case.* Leiden, E. J. Brill, 1966.

Boxer, C. R.: *The Christian Century in Japan, 1549–1650.* Berkeley, University of California Press, 1951.

————: "The Affairs of the *Madre de Deus,* A Chapter in the History of the Portuguese in Japan." *Transactions of the Japan Society* (London), XXVI (1929), 4–94.

Branley, Brendan R.: *Christianity and the Japanese.* New York, Maryknoll, 1966.

Brunner, Emil: "The Unique Christian Mission: The *Mukyōkai* ('Non-Church') Movement in Japan." *Religion and Culture Essays in Honor of Paul Tillich,* ed. Walter Leibrecht, New York, 1959, pp. 287–90.

Cary, Otis: *A History of Christianity in Japan.* 2 vols. New York, Fleming H. Revell, 1909.

Claudius, John (ed.): *A Golden Jubilee, 1865–1915; General View of Catholicism in Japan.* Nagasaki, 1914.

Clement, Ernest W.: *Christianity in Modern Japan.* Philadelphia, American Baptist Publication Society, 1905.

Faust, Allen Klein: *Christianity as a Social Factor in Modern Japan.* Lancaster, Steinman & Foltz, 1909.

Fullerton, Georgiana: *Laurentia: A Tale of the Jesuit Missions in Japan.* London, Burns & Oates, 1883.

Germany, Charles H.: *Protestant Theologies in Modern Japan; A History of Dominant Theological Currents from 1920–1960.* Tokyo, IISR Press, 1965.

Greene, Daniel Crosby (ed.): *The Christian Movement in Japan.* Tokyo, Methodist Publishing House, 1906.

Hatano, Seiichi: *Time and Eternity.* Tr. I. Suzuki. National Commission for UNESCO, 1961.

Hine, Leland D.: *Axling; a Christian Presence in Japan.* Valley Forge, Pa., Judson Pr., 1969.

Hiraga, Gen'ichi: "The Trend of Studies of 'Kirishitan' Literature," *Acta Asiatica* (Bulletin of the Institute of Eastern Culture, No. 4; Tokyo, 1963), pp. 97–113.

Iglehart, Charles W.: *A Century of Protestant Christianity in Japan.* Tokyo & Rutland, Vt., Charles E. Tuttle, 1960.

Laures, Johannes: *The Catholic Church in Japan.* Tokyo & Rutland, Vt., Charles E. Tuttle, 1954.

Michalson, Carl: *Japanese Contributions to Christian Theology*. Philadelphia, Westminster Press, 1960.

Natori, Junichi: *Historical Stories of Christianity in Japan*. Tokyo, Hokuseidô, 1957.

Paske-Smith, M. (ed.): *Japanese Traditions of Christianity*. Kobe, J. L. Thompson, 1930.

Powles, Cyril H.: "Abe Isoo and the Role of Christians in the Founding of the Japanese Socialist Movement, 1895–1905." *Harvard Yenching Papers on Japan* (Harvard Yenching Institute, 1961).

Saitô, Sôichi: *A Study of the Influence of Christianity upon Japanese Culture*. Tokyo, Japan Council of the Institute of Pacific Relations, 1931.

Scheiner, Irwin: *Christian Converts and Social Protest in Meiji Japan*. Berkeley, University of California Press, 1970.

Schull, William J.: "The Effect of Christianity on Consanguinity in Nagasaki," *American Anthropologist,* LV (January–March, 1959), 74–88.

Schwantes, Robert S.: "Christianity *versus* Science: A Conflict of Ideas in Meiji Japan" (Religion and Modernization in the Far East: A symposium, I), *FEO,* XII (No. 2, February, 1957), 123–32.

Spae, Joseph John: "The Catholic Church in Japan," *Contemporary Religions in Japan,* IV (No. 1, March, 1963), 3–78.

Thomas, W. T.: *Protestant Beginnings in Japan*. Tokyo & Rutland, Vt., Charles E. Tuttle, 1959.

Tillich, Paul: *Christianity and the Encounter of the World Religions*. New York, 1961.

Uchimura, Kanzô: *How I Became a Christian,* Tokyo, Keiseisha, 1908.

Van Kecken, Joseph L.: *The Catholic Church in Japan since 1859*. Tr. & rev. by John van Hoydonck. Tokyo, Enderle, 1963.

New Religions

Ariga, Tetsutarô: "The So-called 'Newly-Arisen Sects' in Japan," Missionary Research Library, *Occasional Bulletin,* Vol. V, No. 4, March, 1954.

Brannen, Noah S.: *Sôka Gakkai; Japan's Militant Buddhists*. Richmond, J. Knox, 1968.

Dator, James Allen: *Sôkagakkai, Builders of the Third Civilization; American and Japanese Members*. Seattle, University of Washington, 1969.

Fujiwara, Hirotatsu: *I Denounce Soka Gakkai*. Tr. by Worth C. Grant. Tokyo, Nisshin Hôdô, 1970.

Hammer, R. J.: *Japan's New Religions Frontier,* London, SCM Press, 1962.

Ikeda, Daisaku: *The Human Revolution*. 4 vols. Tokyo, Seikyo Press 1968.

International Institute for the Study of Religions (ed.): *Religion and Modern Life*. Tokyo, IISR, 1958.

International Institute for the Study of Religions (ed.): *Contemporary Religion in Japan*. Vol. 1-Nos. 1–4, Vol.2-Nos. 1–4. Tokyo, IISR, 1960–1962.

McFarland, Neill H.: "The New Religions of Japan," *The Perkins School of Theology Journal,* Vol. XIII, No. 1. 1958.

Murata, Kiyoaki: *Japan's New Buddhism; An Objective Account of Soka Gakkai*. Tokyo, Walker Weatherhill, 1969.

Offner, Clark B.: *Modern Japanese Religions; with Special Emphasis upon their Doctrines of Healing*. New York, Twayne, 1963.

Risshô Kôseikai: *Risshô Kôseikai*. Tokyo, RK, 1966.

Schiffer, Wilhelm: "New Religions in Postwar Japan," *Monumenta Nipponica,* XI (No. 1. 1, April, 1955), 1–14.

Tenrikyô, The Headquarters of.: *A Short History of Tenrikyô*. Tenri, Nara-ken, Headquarters of Tenrikyo Church, 1956.

Thomsen, Harry: *The New Religions of Japan*. Tokyo & Rutland, Vt., Charles E. Tuttle, 1963.

Yuasa, Tatsuki: "PL (Perfect Liberty)," *Contemporary Religions in Japan,* I (No. 3, September, 1960), 20–29.

Folk Religion

Basabe, Fernando M.: *Japanese Youth Confronts Religion; a Sociological Survey*. Tokyo, Sophia University (*Monumenta Nipponica* Monograph), 1967.

Batchelor, John: *The Ainu and Their Folklore*. London, Religious Tract Society, 1901.

Buchanan, Daniel C.: "Inari, Its Origin, Development, and Nature," *TASJ*, Second Series, XII (1935), 1–191.

Buckley, Edmund: *Phallicism in Japan*. Chicago, University Chicago, 1895.

Casal, V. A.: "The Goblin, Fox and Badger and Other Witch Animals of Japan," *Folklore Studies*, XVIII (1959), 1–94.

Earhart, H. Byron: *A Religious Study of the Mount Haguro Sect of Shugendô; an Example of Japanese Mountain Religion*. Tokyo, Sophia University, 1970.

Fairchild, William P.: "Shamanism in Japan," *Folklore Studies*, XXI (1962), 1–122.

Harada, Toshiaki: "The Development of Matsuri," *Philosophical Studies of Japan*, Vol. II, comp. Japanese National Commission for UNESCO (Tokyo, 1961), pp. 99–117.

Hori, Ichirô: *Folk Religion in Japan; Continuity and Change*. Tokyo, University of Tokyo Press, 1968.

Ouwenhand, C.: *Namazu-e and their Themes; an Interpretative Approach to Some Aspects of Japanese Folk Religion*. Leiden, Brill, 1964.

Satow, E. M.: "The Mythology and Religious Worship of the Ancient Japanese," *The Westminster and Foreign Quarterly Review*, New Series, LIX (1881), 27–57.

Saunders, E. Dale: "Japanese Mythology," *Mythologies of the Ancient World*, ed. Samuel Noah Kramer (Garden City, 1961), pp. 409–442.

———: "On the Ainu Term 'Kamui,' " *TASJ*, XVI (1899), 17–32.

———: "Ancient Japanese Rituals," *TASJ*, VII, Part I (1879), 97–132; IX (1881), 182–211.

Japanese Learned Societies Related to the Study of Religion

RELIGION IN GENERAL

Kokusai Shûkyô Kenkyûjo (International Institute for the Studies of Religions)
Sophia University, Kioi-cho, Chiyoda-ku, Tokyo. Tel: (812)2111, Ext. 2343. *International Religious News; Contemporary Religions in Japan.*

Nippon Chûsei Tetsugakukai (The Japan Society of Medieval Philosophy)
c/o Sophia University, Kioi-cho, Chiyoda-ku, Tokyo. Tel: (263)6267. *Chûsei Shisô Kenkyû* (Studies in Medieval Thought), annual in Japanese.

Nippon Rinri Gakkai (The Japanese Society for Ethics)
c/o Department of Ethics, Faculty of Literature, University of Tokyo, Hongo 7, Bunkyo-ku, Tokyo. Tel: (812)2111, Ext. 3372. *Rinrigaku Nempô* (Annals of Ethics), annual in Japanese.

Nippon Shûkyô Gakkai (Japanese Association for Religious Studies)
c/o Faculty of Literature, University of Tokyo, Hongo 7, Bunkyo-ku, Tokyo. Tel: (812)2111, Ext. 2343. *Journal of Religious Studies* (Shûkyô Kenkyû), quarterly in Japanese; *Religion East and West,* annual in English.

Nippon Tetsugakukai (The Philosophical Association of Japan)
c/o Department of Philosophy, Faculty of Literature, Hôsei University, Fujimi 2, Chiyoda-ku, Tokyo. Tel: (262) 2351. *Tetsugaku* (Philosophy), annual in Japanese.

Shûkyôgaku Kenkyûkai (The Society for the Study of Religions)
c/o University of Tokyo, Hongo 7, Bunkyo-ku, Tokyo. Tel: (812)
2111, Ext. 2343. *Shûkyôgaku Zasshi* (Journal of the Study of Religions),
annual in Japanese.

Taishô Daigaku Shûkyô Kenkyûjo (The Institute of Religion, Taishô
University)
c/o Taishô University, Nishisugamo, Toshima-ku, Tokyo. Tel: (918)
7311. *Shûkyôgaku Nempô* (The Annual of Science of Religion), annual
in Japanese.

Tôhô Gakkai (The Institute of Eastern Culture)
Nishikanda 2, Chiyoda-ku, Tokyo. Tel: (261)1061, (262)7221.
Tôhôgaku (Eastern Studies), bi-annual in Japanese; *Acta Asiatica,*
Bulletin of the Institute of Eastern Culture, bi-annual in English;
Books and Articles on Oriental Subjects Published in Japan, annual in
English & Japanese; *Transactions of International Conference of Orientalists
in Japan,* annual in Japanese & English.

SHINTÔ

Shintô Gakkai (The Society of Shintô Studies)
c/o Izumo Oyashiro Tokyo Bunshi, Roppongi 7, Minato-ku, Tokyo.
Tel: (401)9301. *Shintô Gaku* (Review of Shintô Studies), quarterly in
Japanese.

Shintô Shûkyô Gakkai (The Society of Shintô Studies)
c/o Department of Shintô, Faculty of Literature, Kokugakuin University, Higashi 4, Shibuya-ku, Tokyo. Tel: (409)0111, Ext. 373.
Shintô Shûkyô, (Journal of Shintô Studies), quarterly in Japanese.

BUDDHISM

Bukkyô Bungaku Kenkyûkai (Society for Studies of Buddhist Literature)
c/o Mr. Kobayashi, Ôtsuka Sakashita-machi 90, Bunkyô-ku, Tokyo.
Tel: (941)5264. *Bukkyô Bungaku Kenkyû* (Studies of Buddhist Literature); *Bukkyô Bungaku Kenkyûkaihô* (Proceedings of the Society for
Studies of Buddhist Literature).

Bukkyô Gakkai (Society of Buddhist Studies)

c/o Komazawa University, Fukazawa-chô, Setagaya-ku, Tokyo. Tel: (421)8151. *Bukkyô Gakkaishi* (Journal of the Society of Buddhist Studies).

Bukkyô Kenkyûjo (Institution of Buddhim, Faculty of Buddhism, Risshô University)

c/o Risshô University, Higashi Ôsaki, Shinagawa-ku, Tokyo. Tel: (491)9317. *Ôsaki Gakuhô* (Report from Ôsaki).

Bukkyô Kenkyûjo (Buddhist Research Institute)

c/o Ryûkoku University, Omiya Shichijo, Shimokyo-ku, Kyoto. Tel: (361)7351. *Bukkyô Kenkyû* (Studies in Buddhism).

Bukkyôshi Gakkai (The Society of the History of Buddhism)

c/o Heirakuji Shoten, Higashitôir.dôri Sanjô Noboru, Nakakyô-ku, Kyoto. Tel: (221)0016. *Bukkyô Shigaku* (The Journal of the History of Buddhism).

Indo Bukkyô Gakkai (The Society for Indic and Buddhist Studies)

c/o Kyoto University, Yoshidahon-machi, Sakyô-ku, Kyoto. Tel: (771)8111, Ext. 68. *Miscellanea Indologica Kiotiensia.*

Jôdo Gakkai (Association of Jôdo Theory)

c/o Taishô University, Nishisugamo, Toshima-ku, Tokyo. Tel: (918) 7311. *Jôdo Gaku* (Jôdo Theory).

Jôdo Kenkyûkai (The Society of Pure Land Studies, Bukkyô University)

c/o Bukkyô University, Shino Kitahanabo-machi, Kita-ku, Kyoto. Tel: (491)0236. *Jôdo Kenkyû* (Journal of Pure Land Studies).

Mikkyô Gakkai (The Esoteric Buddhist Society)

c/o Kôyasan University, Koya-machi, Izu-gun, Wakayama-ken. Tel: 2921. *Mikkyô Bunka* (Esoteric Buddhist Culture).

Nippon Bukkyô Gakkai (The Japan Buddhist Research Association)

c/o Ôtani University, Koyama Kamifusa-cho, Kita-ku, Kyoto. Tel: (441)4104, Ext. 27. *Nippon Bukkyô Gakkai Nempô* (Journal of the Japan Buddhist Research Association), annual in Japanese.

Nippon Bukkyô Kenkyûkai (The Japan Buddhist Research Association) c/o Hanazono University, Hanazono Kitsuji Kitamachi, Ukyô-ku, Kyoto. Tel: (463)7171. *Nihon Bukkyô Kenkyû* (The Journal of the Nippon Buddhist Research), annual in Japanese.

Nippon Indo-gaku Bukkyô Gakkai (Japanese Association of Indian and Buddhist Studies)

c/o Faculty of Literature, University of Tokyo, Hongô 7, Bunkyô-ku, Tokyo. Tel: (812)2111, Ext. 2348. Indogaku *Bukkyô-gaku Kenkyû* (Journal of Indian and Buddhist Studies), bi-annual in English & Japanese.

Ôtani Daigaku Bukkyô Kenkyûkai (Ôtani University Buddhist Research Association)

c/o Ôtani University, Koyama Kamifusa-cho, Kita-ku, Kyoto. Tel: (441)4104. *Bukkyô Kenkyû* (Buddhist Seminar), annual in Japanese.

Ôtani Daigaku Shinshû Gakkai (The Ôtani Society for Studies of Shinshû Buddhism)

c/o Ôtani University, Koyama Kamifusa-chô, Kita-ku, Kyoto. Tel: (441)4104.

• **Ryûkoku Daigaku Shinshû Gakkai** (The Ryûkoku Society of Shinshû Buddhist Studies)

c/o Ryûkoku University Library, Ômiya Shichijô, Shimokyô-ku, Kyoto. Tel: (361)7351. *Shinshûgaku* (Shinshû Studies).

Shinshû Rengo Gakkai (Shinshû Societies of Buddhist Studies)

c/o Ôtani University, Koyama Kamifusa-chô, Kita-ku, Kyoto. Tel: (441)4104. *Shinshû Kenkyû* (Shinshû Buddhist Studies).

Tendai Kenkyûkai (Association of Tendai Studies)

c/o Taishô University, Nishisugamo, Toshima-ku, Tokyo. Tel: (918) 7311. *Tendai Gakuhô* (Proceedings of Tendai Studies).

Tôhoku Indogaku Shûkyô Gakkai (Tôhoku Association of Indian and Religious Studies)

c/o Tôhoku University, Katahira-chô, Sendai. Tel: (27)6200, Ext. 2353. *Tôhoku Indogaku-Shûkyôgakkai Gakuhô* (Proceedings of the Tôhoku Association of Indian and Religious Studies).

Tôkai Indogaku-Bukkyô Gakkai (Tôkai Association of Indian and Buddhist Studies) c/o Nagoya University, Furô-cho, Chigusa-ku, Nagoya. Tel: (781) 5111, Ext. 2217. *Tôkai Bukkyô* (Journal of Tôkai Buddhist Studies).

Zengaku Kenkyûkai (Society for Studies in Zen Buddhism)
c/o Hanazono University, Hanazono, Ukyô-ku, Kyoto. Tel: (841) 7171. *Zen Bukkyô Kenkyû* (Studies in Zen Buddhism).

CHRISTIANITY

Aoyama Gakuin Kirisutokyô Gakkai (Society of Christian Study, Aoyama Gakuin University)
c/o Aoyama Gakuin University, Shibuya, Shibuya-ku, Tokyo. Tel: (402)8111. *Kirisutokyô Ronshû* (The Journal of Christian Studies), annual in Japanese.

Kirishitan Bunka Kenkyûkai (Association for the Study of Early Kirishitan Culture)
c/o Sophia University, Kioi-chô, Chiyoda-ku, Tokyo. Tel: (265)9211. *Kirishitan Kenkyû* (Kirishitan Studies); *Kirishitan Bunka Kenkyûkai Kaihô* (Proceedings of Kirishitan Culture Studies).

Kirisutokyô Kenkyûkai (Society of Studies in the Christian Religion)
c/o Dôshisha University, Sôkokuji Monzen-chô, Kamikyô-ku, Kyoto. Tel: (211)2311. *Kirisutokyô Kenkyû* (Studies in the Christian Religion), Annual in Japanese.

Kirisutokyô Shakaimondai Kenkyûkai, Dôshisha Daigaku Jimmon Kagaku Kenkyûjo (Study Committee of Christianity and Social Problems)
c/o Dôshisha University, Imaidegawadôri Karasuma Higashi Hairu, Kamikyô-ku, Kyoto. Tel: (211)2311. *Kirisutokyô Shakaimondai Kenkyû* (Study of Christianity and Social Problems).

Kirisutokyô Shigakkai (The Society of Historical Studies of Christianity)
c/o Kantô Gakuin University, Miharudai, Minami-ku, Yokohama. Tel: (231)1001. *Kirisutokyô Shigaku* (The Journal of History of Christianity), annual in Japanese.

Nippon Kirisutokyô Gakkai (Japan Association of Research on Christianity) c/o Kantô Gakuin University, Mutsuura, Kanazawa-ku, Yokohama. Tel: (781)2008. *Nippon no Shingaku* (Theological Studies in Japan), annual in Japanese.

Nippon Kyûyaku Gakkai (Society for Old Testament Studies)
c/o Tokyo Union Theological Seminary, Mitaka, Tokyo.

Nippon Shinyaku Gakkai (Society for New Testament Studies)
c/o Theological School, Kansei Gakuin University, Nishinomiya.

Rikkyô Daigaku Kirisutokyô Gakkai (The Society for Christian Studies, Rikkyô University)
c/o Rikkyô University, Ikebukuro, Toshima-ku, Tokyo.

Tokyo Shingaku Daigaku Shingakkai (Society for Theological Studies, Tokyo Union Theological Seminary)
c/o Tokyo Union Theological Seminary, Mitaka, Tokyo.

SHINGAKU

Sekimonshingakkai (Society of Sekimonshingaku Studies)
c/o Mr. Ishikawa, Zôshigaya 6-1146, Toshima-ku, Tokyo. Tel: (971) 5693. *Kokoro* (Heart).

TAOISM

Dôkyô Gakkai (Institution for Taoistic Research)
c/o Waseda University, Toyama-chô, Shinjuku-ku, Tokyo. Tel: (409) 0111. *Tôho Shûkyô* (The Journal of Eastern Religion), bi-annual in Japanese.

ISLAMIC STUDIES

Nippon Islam Kyôkai (Association for Islamic Studies in Japan)
c/o Waseda University, Toyama-chô, Shinjuku-ku, Tokyo. Tel: (203) 4111. *Islam Sekai* (The World of Islam), annual in Japanese.

TIBETAN STUDIES

Nippon Tibet Gakkai (Japanese Association for Tibetan Studies)
c/o Kansai University, Yamate-machi, Suita-shi, Osaka. Tel: (381)1954. *Nippon Tibet Gakkai Kaihô* (Report of the Japanese Association for Tibetan Studies).

Japanese Life and Culture Series

Distributor: JAPAN PUBLICATIONS TRADING COMPANY
Addresses: *JAPAN*—P.O. Box 5030, Tokyo International.
U.S.A.—1255 Howard Street, San Francisco, Calif.,
94103.
In Australia and New Zealand order directly from:
Paul Flesch & Co. Pty. Ltd.
259 Collins St., Melbourne, Australia, 3000.

ANESAKI Masaharu: *Religious Life of the Japanese People.* 122pp.
Soft cover $3.00; Hard cover $4.75
In Japan one finds a curious mixture of native Shintoism, Indian Buddhism, Chinese Confucianism and Western Christianity. This book was written by one of Japan's most honored scholars and first published during the strident nationalistic period before World War II, showing that even then Japan contained a strong humanistic and moral force. Kishimoto Hideo, former professor and director of the Tokyo University Library, has revised the book to bring it up to date and indicate the postwar changes in Japanese religious life.

INOUE Mitsusada: *Introduction to Japanese History before the Meiji Restoration.* 151pp. $3.00
The author, professor of history of the University of Tokyo offers a succinct account of the history of Japan until the mid-nineteenth century. Inoue is the author of the work *The Origin of the Japanese Nation* which is considered one of the most authoritative in this field.

ISIDA Ryuziro: *The Geography of Japan.* 124pp. $3.00
This is an introduction to the varied and complex geography of Asia's most productive country. Here one can see in graphic form the small percentage of arable land, the reason Japan must import some food and raw materials and export manufactured goods.

The author, professor emeritus of geography at Hitotsubashi University, discusses these and other important issues: climate; population problems; resources and industries; agriculture; fisheries; foreign trade; natural disasters; and regional planning for development.

K.B.S. ed.: *Synopses of Contemporary Japanese Literature II, 1936–1955.* 231pp. Soft cover $3.75; Hard cover $5.75

Synopses of selected Japanese literary works, one from each author, written in the years 1936–1955, with short biographical sketches of the writers. Together with Nakamura Mitsuo's *Contemporary Japanese Fiction* in this series, this book will provide necessary outlines of major literary works of this period.

KAIGO Tokiomi: *Japanese Education, its Past and Present.* 128pp. $3.00

Before the foundation of the present system, there were already distinct educational institutions which reflected the spirit and concern of the different periods of Japanese history: (a) education of the nobility (710–1192); (b) education of warriors (1192–1600); (c) education under the Tokugawa shogunate (1600–1868). The author then makes a survey of the development of all levels and branches of the present system: primary, secondary and higher, before dealing with the very advanced field of social education and the problems of modernizing school administration.

KAWAZOE Noboru: *Contemporary Japanese Architecture.* 106pp. $3.00

This is a hundred years' retrospect of the development of modern architecture. It includes much background information essential to an understanding of the social aspect of modern construction industry in a rapidly growing country.

KISHIBE Shigeo: *The Traditional Music of Japan.* 124pp. $3.00
The author, a professor of the University of Tokyo, is one of the leading musicologists in Japan, making comparative studies of Japanese and other Asian music. His study in eighth century Chinese music of the T'ang dynasty brought new light to the

historiography of Asian music. After a succinct account of the history and characteristics of Japanese music, he depicts in outline the major genres such as Gagaku, Shômyô, Biwa music, Noh, Sôkyoku, Shamisen music, Shakuhachi music, folk songs and folk music. The illustrations of the instruments, musicians and scores are very valuable for the students of Japanese music.

NAKAMURA Hajime: *A History of the Development of Japanese Thought* in 2 vols. Vol. 1: 149pp.; Vol. 2: 159pp. $3.00 each

The author is professor of Hindu Philosophy at the University of Tokyo. He opened a new horizon of comparative study of Asian thought when he wrote *The Ways of Thinking of Eastern Peoples: India – Tibet – Japan* (English edition, 1964).

NAKAMURA Mitsuo: *Modern Japanese Fiction, 1868–1926.* Part I: 120pp., Part II: 56pp. $3.00

This book was originally published in two separate volumes entitled *Japanese Fiction in the Meiji Era* and *Japanese Fiction in the Taisho Era.* The author is presently professor of literature at Meiji University. As a critic, dramatist and novelist, he has played a leading role in various fields of Japanese literary activity.

NAKAMURA Mitsuo: *Contemporary Japanese Fiction, 1926–1968.* 168pp. $3.00

In this book, the author of *Modern Japanese Fiction* listed above deals with the development of Japanese fiction of the Shôwa period which is marked by a series of contemporary writers such as Kawabata, Mishima, etc. The two volumes will cover the past hundred years' progress of Japanese literary activites.

OHNO Susumu: *The Origin of the Japanese Language.* 154pp.

Soft cover $3.00; Hard cover $4.75

In this book, the author, professor of Japanese language at Gakushûin University, clarifies the derivations of both Japanese language and race, exercising his pragmatic and factual knowledge of the neighbouring languages and peoples.

Takahashi Masao: *Modern Japanese Economy Since 1868.* 170pp.
$3.00

The book is based on a series of lectures Dr. Takahashi gave at Kyushu University in the spring semester of 1963 for visiting students from Asian countries. Staring from the steps leading to the Meiji Restoration, he gives a thoroughgoing account of the formation of capitalism, the social, economical development between the two wars, and the changes after World War II, with a description of post-war Japanese economy.

Toyoda Takeshi: *A History of Pre-Meiji Commerce in Japan.* 106pp.
$3.00

The author is presently a professor of Japanese history at Tôhoku University, Sendai. His books, *Japanese Feudal Cities* and *Medieval Japanese Commerce,* are remarkable contributions to the study of feudal commerce and social structure of Japan.

Tuge Hideomi: *Historical Development of Science and Technology in Japan.* 219pp. $3.00

Tuge, professor of Hosei University, traces how Japanese science developed first under the influence of Chinese culture and later, in increasing degree, under that of Western science. The description comes down to 1957 when Japan joined the International Geophysical Year Programme and sent the vessel ' SOYA-MARU" to the South Pole. The *Addenda* give more recent information.

Ushiomi Toshitaka: *Forestry and Mountain Village Communities in Japan.* 118pp. $3.00

Being one of the few books in English on this subject, this work gives a thorough picture of the development and growth of forestry and mountain-community life since the mid-nineteenth century, when the lands of the feudal lords passed into the hand of the new government of Meiji. It also relates the sufferings of the people caused by the bureaucratic setups of the time, and how democratic ideals have been brought into such areas after World War II. The author is a noted scholar of civil law and sociology at the University of Tokyo.

Watanabe Shoko: *Japanese Buddhism, a Critical Appraisal.* 174pp.
$3.00

This is the first attempt in English to define critically the social and theological significance of Japanese Buddhism. The author, well-known linguist and Buddhist scholar, presents a clear-cut evaluation, both positive and negative, of Buddhism as it manifests itself in Japan.

NEW BOOKS, 1971

Inoura Yoshinobu: *A History of Japanese Theater I.*   pp.

The lineages of the major theatrical arts of the ancient and medieval Japan such as Gigaku, Bugaku, Ennen Noh, Sarugaku Noh, Dengaku Noh, Shungen Noh up to the establishment of Nohgaku (Noh and Kyogen) are systematically reviewed.

Kawatake Toshio: *A History of Japanese Theater II.*   pp.

The author describes the origin and development of the Tokugawa Theater represented by Bunraku and Kabuki.